WHEN GIRLS FALL OUT

A GUIDE FOR PARENTS OF DAUGHTERS TOLD FROM THE GIRLS' POINT OF VIEW

Andrew, Holly and Naomi Hampton

ACKNOWLEDGEMENTS

I am grateful to literally thousands of people who have helped shape the ideas in this book. The hundreds of teachers I have trained, the thousands of girls I have workshopped with and the many school leaders and other influencers who have shown genuine interest in finding a better way to empower girls.

In particular, I am grateful to the Governors of Thorpe Hall School, Essex, who have consistently encouraged and supported the development of Girls on Board since it was originally conceived in 2011. They allowed me to take time away from my leadership role at the school to develop my ideas and ultimately spread the word across the world.

Finally, I would like to thank my family, my two daughters, my son, and my wife for listening to me witter on about this topic for many years.

Andrew Hampton

Published and distributed by Girls on Board Ltd, 103 Marine Parade, Leigh-on-Sea, SS9 2JR

Andrew, Holly and Naomi Hampton have asserted their rights under the Copyright, Designs and Patents Act, 1988, to be identified as Author of this work. No part of this publication may be reproduced or transmitted in any form or by any means, electronic or mechanical, including photocopying, recording, or any information storage or retrieval system, without prior permission in writing from the publishers.

Andrew, Holly and Naomi Hampton

First published in Great Britain 2021

ISBN 978-1-3999-0108-6

Andrew Hampton is the father of two daughters and a son. He has been a teacher for 35 years and a Headteacher for 18 of those. He has taught in and led coeducational schools which educate girls and boys from age 2 to 16.

Holly Hampton is Andrew's younger daughter who lived through the normal friendship turbulence experienced by girls at school, with her father as Headteacher. She graduated from the University of Cambridge and now works as a lawyer.

Dr Naomi Hampton is Andrew's older daughter and has contributed her personal experiences of friendship turbulence as well as what she has learned about human relationships through her work as a Psychiatrist. She graduated from the University of Oxford and now works for the NHS.

FOREWORD

In our experience, nearly every school-age girl will experience problems with friendships at some point; it is a normal part of growing up. The majority of girls will identify with difficulties in making and maintaining friends, feeling left out or not popular enough. Trying to find the best way to support upset daughters seems to be a core feature of modern parenting. This book is born out of the authors' direct experiences – Holly and Naomi as women who went through it and Andrew as a father, teacher and Headteacher of girls for 35 years. What we are saying in this book is what we have been told by girls themselves.

When Girls Fall Out is a book for the adults involved in supporting girls. The book brings all the adults together to understand girl friendships, from the girls' point of view.

In writing this book we wanted to help as wide an audience as possible to understand the issues faced by girls when they fall out with each other. When trying to support girls in conflict, it is not uncommon for the adults to fall out with one another too! That might be the parents from the different families whose girls are involved in a squabble, or it might be parents and teachers falling out over the best way to help the girls get through some tough times.

We don't pull any punches in this book. Both teachers and parents will read things here that are overtly critical of strategies they have commonly used to support girls. Whilst these adult-led resolution methods may well be employed with the best intentions, they often lead to only short-lived and superficial harmony. We believe that by gaining a strong understanding of the girls' point of view, families and teachers can better help girls to resolve friendship issues for themselves.

The first part of the book focuses on parenting and seeing that role from the girls' point of view. The latter part of the book focuses on the school-based approach called Girls on Board. Girls on Board empowers girls to resolve their friendship issues for themselves, through empathy-evoking workshops and sessions. Andrew created Girls on Board in 2011 while Headteacher at Thorpe Hall School, Essex. The approach has gained many awards and nominations since then and has been adopted by schools throughout the world; it is seen as a major contributor to girls' mental health and wellbeing. 10 years later over 50,000 girls had benefitted from their schools adopting the approach and that number continues to grow.

We want to emphasise that this book does not seek to stereotype female behaviour or present a reductive view of complex individual relationships. We fully recognise that girls are unique individuals, have different needs, interests and desires and come with a multitude of experiences and backgrounds. We make generalised observations which can never ring true for every girl; we are aware of numerous exceptions to the rule. However, drawing from our experience, reference to psychological research and collaboration with hundreds of schools, undeniable patterns of behaviour have emerged. Observing and working with these patterns has allowed us to draw out commonalities that apply to the majority of girls aged 7-18 and these have proved extremely useful in helping girls understand and resolve their friendship issues for themselves.

We make many assertions in the book about the way things are for girls and their friendships. Many of these assertions are backed up by research but rather than add citations every time, we have summarised the research in Appendix 3 at the end of the book. Generally speaking, when we talk about girls we are referring to girls between the ages of 7 and 18 and the reason for that is explained in the book.

We make much use of storytelling in this book and these stories are all fictional; any resemblance they may have to actual people or events is coincidental.

Contents

Why is this book about girls and not boys?

One of the key developmental tasks for both boys and girls of school-age is learning to create and foster significant social relationships. Girls place a high value on intimacy, which makes them awesome friends and fearsome enemies. They form such close friendships that it can be very painful when things go wrong. While boy friendships can be just as intense, they often (though not always) operate more in the realm of competition and action, rather than closeness and confidentiality. When girls fall out it seems to hurt more than when boys fall out. On the whole boys tend to find resolution to their conflicts relatively quickly – perhaps because their friendships are often not as intimate - and adult support or intervention is not normally needed. When it comes to friendship, boys and girls are different.

When Girls Fall Out is about girls because there are significant differences in the ways parents need to support their daughters compared to the way they support their sons. Why these differences exist is a huge and fascinating question. While we will touch on aspects of these gender differences, a full exploration is beyond the scope of this book.

There are moments in the book when the behavioural characteristics of girls is shown to be heavily influenced by things adults regard as trivial. Many of these moments may well be true also of boys, but we will not always point that out because... well, because this book is about girls.

CHAPTER ONE

Parents and daughters

When girls fall out:
- it is different to when boys fall out
- it can feel like the end of the world for them
- parents can feel powerless, anxious and worried
- teachers rarely succeed in making things consistently better

From the moment she emerges into the world, a child is engaged in a slow and protracted negotiation to establish her unique identity. In what way and to what extent will she adopt the ways of her parent and how much will she strike out on her own? Each child will take a different journey and outcomes can vary greatly, even within a single family. Every aspect of life has to be negotiated, and at each stage of childhood and adolescence the negotiations can re-open suddenly and without warning. Whilst we understand that each major shift in maturity is a rite of passage for the child, we sometimes forget that as a child grows and their parenting needs change, this is equally a rite of passage for the parent.

That moment when she decides to take the bus, or walk to school with her friends, represents an irreversible moment of separation for the parent. Each such moment symbolises the inevitable approach of the time when the daughter no longer relies on her parent for her physical needs. Although a daughter's growing ability to look after herself can bring new freedoms for her parent, when it comes to her emotional self-reliance it can be more difficult for the parent to let go. As a daughter gains more independence, her life will also be growing in emotional complexity. As much as anything it is hard for a parent to see their daughter go through tough times emotionally and realise that the problem cannot be easily 'fixed'. Parents can support through listening and sympathy, but actively trying to remove the causes of upset will simply inhibit their daughter's long-term emotional growth and resilience. Instead, it is essential that parents develop and demonstrate their trust and belief in their daughter's own abilities to navigate emotional turmoil.

While it may be straightforward to solve a squabble over a toy at a playgroup, as the daughter grows up, the ability of the parent to intervene successfully when friendship issues arise is diminished. Parental involvement can then become interfering rather than supportive; it is neither neutral nor risk-free. Neither parents, nor teachers for that matter, can 'fix' the problems when girls fall out. This book will demonstrate how their advice, their words, their actions - however well intentioned - are at best mildly effective and at worst disastrous.

Scenario

Let's start with a common tale of the tangles, fallouts and insecurities, experienced everyday by girls at school.

Ava is unhappy. Ava feels she is being left out because her good friend **Beth** only wants to *hang out with* new-girl **Dita**.

As she arrives on the playground at break time, Ava sees Dita beckoning to Beth to come over and join her. As Beth sets off to join Dita, she pulls Ava along with her. Ava is wary of Dita and doesn't want to become a group of three with her and Beth; but she goes along anyway. Ava's fears are confirmed as Beth and Dita discover many shared interests and make each other laugh.

Ava feels abandoned and that her friendship with Beth is under threat from Dita. In an attempt to regain control she sends Dita a text that evening, which says:

Ava (to Dita): *No offence but I'm asking Beth for a sleepover on Saturday. Mum says I can only have 1 person – soz.*

When Dita gets this text she copies it to Beth straight away, and they begin a text thread, which reads:

Beth: *Omg that's so mean of Ava. Her mum would never say that. Anyway, everyone is so tired of Ava's "vegan sleepover" thing LOL*
Dita: *I know right, it's so attention seeking*

Dita's older brother sees this text thread and copies it to Ava's brother, who shows it to Ava. Ava is shocked: Beth has called her mean and has made fun of her veganism and Dita has called her attention seeking. She plots to disrupt Beth's new friendship, and texts Dita:

Ava (to Dita): *Beth told me that you think that I am attention seeking – if you've got a problem u should say it to my face next time. btw Beth thinks u r really two-faced.*

This text unsettles Dita who doesn't want to get caught up in a friendship drama. Dita texts Beth to say:

Dita (to Beth): *I think Ava is getting a bit clingy and manipulative. Let's hang with the boys tomorrow?*
Beth: *I agree.*

The next day, Ava struggles to find anyone to hang out with; she has a bad day and goes home upset.

Beth and Dita hang out with the boys but Beth feels left out when Dita's banter is much more successful than hers. Dita wants to continue to be friends with the boys and starts to play football with them, but Beth is not comfortable with that and ends up on her own.

Like Ava, Beth goes home, having ended the day friendless, upset and in need of support from her parent.

After exploring Ava's version of the story, Ava's parent tells her off for being aggressive towards Dita in her text, and lying about only being allowed one friend for a sleepover. Her parent feels this is what caused all the upset that followed. Ava's phone is confiscated for three days. This makes Ava feel both abandoned by her parent and betrayed by her friend.

Beth tells her parent that she is being bullied by Ava and Dita because they deliberately exclude her every day. Although this is simply not true, Beth's parent does not question her, but emails the school demanding immediate action and wants sanctions to be taken against Ava and Dita.

The next day, teachers soon realise that Ava and Beth, who used to be good friends, are unhappy. They speculate that the new girl – Dita – may have caused this upset. However, the teachers are largely distracted by having to deal with an aggressive email exchange with Beth's parent, who is unyielding. After some one-to-one conversations with the individual girls, the Head of Year calls all three into her office for a general chat and to try to heal the rifts.

The Head of Year, after listening to three different stories describing the last two days, realises that, despite all the upset, none of the girls has actually done anything wrong or broken a school rule. She tells them that they should all be more resilient, more considerate of each other's feelings and stay off social media.

After the chat with the Head of Year:
- Ava feels that the Head of Year has condoned the behaviour of the other

two in leaving her out, and has failed to sanction Dita for calling her 'attention-seeking' in a text.

- Beth feels guilty that she was quick to turn her back on Ava in favour of new-girl, Dita. She also feels annoyed with herself and embarrassed that she was not able to keep up with Dita in her interaction with the boys. She feels that her parent's interference has led to the Head of Year's intervention and that this will make it doubly hard to make friends again with Ava, which is what she wants. She feels patronised and victimised by the slightly condescending tone of the Head of Year's conclusions, like she is being blamed for something she didn't do.
- Dita is happy that she has found some new friendships amongst the boys which has given her extra credibility amongst other girl groups as well. She is bemused by the remarks of the Head of Year and just assumes that she has been called in by mistake. She regards the other two girls as 'a bit weird' and privately resolves not to hang out with them again.

Of course, the story would not end there! The mediation session held by the Head of Year made things worse. Similarly, the reactions of the parents have been unhelpful and potentially damaging to the vital sense of trust that needs to exist between the child, the school and the parent. Ava's parent's judgmental and disapproving reaction has driven Ava into resolving to seek solace from the family dog in future. Beth feels constantly let down by her parent's over-reactive response to the story of her day. She feels increasingly invisible, numb and alone, unable to find a way to talk to her parent that doesn't make her feel alienated and misunderstood.

As this story shows, small moments of insecurity can quickly escalate into a major fallout. Girls can fall out over things which seem to adults to be low level, trivial and even childish. As adults we can identify with feeling hurt or embarrassed by interactions that may seem trivial when taken out of context. But we are able to draw on experience, self-esteem, social skills, support from others, distraction and our own free-will in order to resolve the majority of these. School-age girls are in the process of developing these complex social skills, calibrating the meaning of interactions and building a sense of perspective. Furthermore, they are doing so while also attending a school setting involving prolonged, close contact with a peer group they have no choice but to coexist with.

A girl may become upset because of the way another girl looked at her, because a friend kept a secret from her, because two friends saw her coming down the corridor and didn't wait for her before going into class, or even because a text was signed off with two rather than three 'x's. To a girl these moments are not trivial because they can all signify a threat to the stability of a friendship. Even the slightest sense that friendships may be lost or damaged can make a girl experience panic and insecurity; that in turn can make her want to find any way possible to regain control and protect her place in the group.

What is vital to understand is:

Every girl must have at least one other girl, in their year group, in their school to call a friend.

Interpersonal relationships are a central part of mental wellbeing for all, adults and children alike. However, as adults our identities are defined by many aspects of our internal and external lives. It is not the same for school-aged girls. Girls' identities are formed through their friendships; it can feel like their friends are who they are. Girls fear isolation and crave reliable, trusting and loyal friendships. Without someone to call 'a friend' on a moment-by-moment basis life can appear bewildering and disconcerting. Being a friendless girl can lead to feelings of abandonment and despair. They can feel misunderstood, powerless and alone.

School is about far more than academia because it is where children learn about social interaction, friendship, conflict, competition and inequality. Within this context, the most important thing is having the comfort of at least one trusted friend to rely on. A friend is the source of consistent external validation at a time in her life when internal validation can be so hard to find.

When a girl arrives at her classroom for the morning registration, she walks through the door and looks around the room. She doesn't so much look for somewhere to sit as whom she might sit next to. If, in her mind, there is no one she feels she can be with, someone who will greet her, smile and make her feel part of a group, then her world can feel as if it is collapsing. Not every girl will be willing and comfortable to admit this but when parents and teachers understand the true significance of this idea, it changes the way they go about supporting girls fundamentally.

This idea that every girl needs a friend is so significant that we call it the Existential Imperative. Understanding how this imperative acts on girls, how it frames their behaviours, attitudes, value systems and their daily lives is one of the core purposes of this book.

Forming friendships

The process of negotiating independence from parents and the acquisition of independent ways of thinking is traditionally associated with adolescence, but in reality it starts much earlier than that.

When it comes to social interactions, parents can mediate their child's friendships to some extent right up until the very first day of school, aged 4. Parents can choose to steer their daughter away from a peer who they consider to be too rough, or who seems not to share the same values of friendships that they themselves hold dear.

When children start school, however, they immediately form relationships with classmates - without the constraints of parental mediation. The adult in the room is a teacher, not a parent. The teacher sets the moral parameters of how friendships will be conducted in the class and on the playground, and then steps back. The children are expected to treat each other as equals, to be fair and kind, not to be mean, abusive or overly physical. Parents may disapprove of some of the friends their daughter is making but any attempt to influence these friendships is rarely supported by the teacher, for whom every child is equally deserving.

With friendships come groups of friends and with groups of friends come allegiances, hierarchy, group identity, mutual support, shared values and experiences and, yes, the potential for conflict. Many of the traits of relational aggression we recognise in pre-teens and teenagers we can also witness in much younger children. From the age of 4, children at school initiate, conduct and enjoy friendships independent of their parent. Parents' knowledge and understanding of each day's social interactions are gained only through the eyes of others who were there at the time. Therefore, try as they might to guide their child through friendship turbulence, parents' ability to 'fix' their child's problems is limited. Just as friendships are formed independently, so the solutions to friendship turbulence are most effectively found independently too.

This chapter has highlighted the challenges girls face in negotiating peer relationships, but we also want to acknowledge and celebrate the independence and strength of girls' friendships too. It is by relying on that independence and strength that parents can empower girls to resolve friendship issues for themselves.

In the next chapter we look in more detail at how friendships are conducted by girls in school.

CHAPTER TWO

Defining the terms of girls' friendships

Coming up in this chapter:
"...the need to blend felt by nearly all girls in school far outweighs the call, from adults, to be individual and proudly different."

In this chapter we look at the rules that apply to friendships between girls at school and the characteristics of typical sizes of groups. This will equip you as a parent to understand your daughter's friendships in greater depth and give you the language to communicate with her effectively.

Explicit and implicit rules
It is useful to see the rules relating to friendships as being either explicit or implicit.

The **explicit rules** are the ones that are stated and re-stated by adults whenever there is conflict in school. These rules are simple and straightforward:

- You must not be mean to people by calling them names, putting them down, leaving them out, keeping secrets or generally upsetting them on purpose.
- You should always do your best to be kind and generous to everyone you come across.

All girls know these rules, they know how to make sure they don't obviously break them, and they know that grown-ups tend to get very agitated when they are broken.

Boys often break the explicit friendship rules of name calling and exclusive behaviour under the guise of banter, but this tends to be reciprocal. Some boys gain notoriety and therefore hierarchical credit by being rebellious with these rules. If a boy calls another boy a cruel name, they tend to respond in kind and don't complain that the explicit friendship rules have been broken. They might be upset, but they don't tell an adult because doing so just leaves them open to more banter. Boys' position in the hierarchy is often determined by how much banter they can withstand. Stereotypically, society tells boys to "man-up" and be tough and ridicules them for showing signs of weakness and sensitivity. This is by no means a desirable pattern of masculinity, but it nonetheless plays out every day in classrooms and playgrounds across the world.

Whilst boys are expected to take social risks and be emotionally thick-skinned, society expects girls to be sensitive and caring. Society shuns aggressive behaviour in women, something we do to the detriment of girls' emotional expression. While name-calling amongst boys may receive a 'tut' or stern look from the teacher on playground duty, a girl being outwardly aggressive in a similar way is likely to receive a harsher reprimand. Breaking the explicit friendship rules is therefore a big deal for girls because they are then regarded as insensitive and uncaring - at odds with societal expectations. This can make them a social outcast.

A girl breaking these rules risks being excluded by others. She loses agency and her power to choose her friends can drain away. Being in trouble with teachers can make her vulnerable to excluding behaviours from any source and any angle.

Even former friends have a tricky choice to make because, by remaining loyal to the girl who broke the rules, they may be tarred by the same brush and become pariahs too.

It is not common for girls to break the explicit rules of friendship; instead their social conflict tends to be played out within the arena of the implicit rules.

Implicit rules.
The implicit rules of friendship are many and complex. They are age-sensitive, context-specific and can also change day-by-day. Implicit rules are a key part of understanding girls' friendships. For instance, the way that girls engage on social media platforms will have its own set of rules, picked up and understood quickly through use. These might pertain to the precise use of particular emojis, punctuation or acronyms, or to acceptable ways to name yourself in your profile.

In younger girls implicit rules can relate to things like the number of times a girl can be allowed to be the one to choose the playground game, or what happens if a girl consistently self-excludes from games as a tactic to draw attention from adults. In older girls, implicit rules might relate to clothing and style; it is acceptable to be influenced by another girl's taste in clothing but not acceptable to get too close to copying it.

Implicit rules, by their nature, are fluid and open to interpretation. They are not enforceable by adults, but breaking these rules will leave a girl vulnerable to disapproval and potentially isolated from her peers. There is, however, a zone which lies within the realm of the implicit rules that also lies close to the explicit rules. It is in this zone that nearly all friendship turbulence occurs and it is where the power dynamics of friendships are defined and played out. The way in which girls manage and manipulate the implicit rules can be very nuanced and the complexity can overwhelm some, especially if they feel they are losing out. To explain this, let's look at an example:

Let's look at a 9-year-old girl whom others regard as bossy on the playground. She does have a tendency to dominate play and choose the games, but not to the extent that she is obviously being unfair or putting others down. She is, in effect, operating in the zone close to the threshold where the breaking of implicit rules tips over into the breaking of explicit rules. If she was to be too dominant and never let anyone else choose the games, then a teacher would be right to tell her off and ask her to share more. She knows this and to protect herself she will have kept in her 'back pocket' instances when other girls chose the game so that she can quote these if challenged by an adult. Her behaviour can be the source of great frustration to others because she **does** dominate the playground games, but she is too clever to be caught out by an adult. This causes other girls to move against her and turbulence within the friendship groups starts to arise.

A girl may feel that the way the implicit rules are being interpreted by others in her group is not working in her favour and she may feel she is not skilled enough or sufficiently empowered to change that. She does have, however, a simple solution that will potentially redress the balance: she can always go to an adult and claim that she is **upset**. By claiming that other girls have upset her she is obliging the adults to become involved and investigate her grounds for complaint. She is requesting that the behaviour of others is no longer scrutinised by peers according to the implicit rules, but by adults according to the explicit rules.

A girl might say, "It's not fair; she always chooses the game and it is always a game I don't like. She is leaving me out." There then follows an investigation by the adults who will attempt to verify and triangulate this statement in the hope that they will find a clear and undeniable truth upon which they can base their next course of action. The result is rarely clear-cut and instances of explicit wrongdoing are usually not found. The adults may sense that some of the implicit rules that relate to the best way to conduct friendships have not been followed but breaking these rules is not actionable. At the end of exhaustive attempts to understand where and how the upset arose, adults will usually conclude matters with a re-statement of the explicit rules with the hope that things will settle down. However, from the girls' point of view, the involvement of adults will have caused fear and resentment; it will have distorted the balance of relations between them and, usually, **everyone is slightly worse off**. Why this is so often the case will be explored further in Chapter 6.

Group Sizes

When girls form friendships they often do so in pairs, threes, fours and sometimes fives or even sixes. Occasionally much larger groups form but it is usually true to say that within the larger group, smaller and more conventionally sized groups co-exist. The bigger the group size the more unwieldy it becomes, leading to obvious issues of organisation and dilemmas about whether social gatherings can legitimately go ahead if not everyone is available. These dilemmas occur less often the smaller the group is.

Some people question why there need to be dilemmas around availability. They argue that no-one 'owns' anyone else and if, for instance, a pair of girls from a group of four or five want to have some exclusive time together then they are fully entitled to do that. However, this argument takes no account of the feelings of the girls in the group who have been left out - be that deliberately or incidentally. It is not that the group can only ever socialise when all members are available, but at the very least there needs to be a discussion and a justification offered as to why a sub-group has made its decision. Without the willingness to be transparent, exclusive behaviour can easily be interpreted as meanness, whether intended or not, and can lead to conflict for all involved.

The advantages and disadvantages of each group size are issues which impact on the moment-by-moment reality of being a girl in school. Talking about group sizes at home can be a great way of gaining insights into how your daughter is thinking and how she views the dynamics and structures of friendship groupings. It will also demonstrate to her that you are interested in and take seriously her understanding of how friendships work.

There is, of course, no ideal group size; they all have advantages and disadvantages.

Pairs

Advantages: There is strength in the idea, 'You can't reject me because without me you would be alone too,' and so the stability of a pair lies in its inter-dependency. There is no risk of being 'left out' in a pair. Most girls agree that the fewer girls there are in a friendship group the closer the bond is between them. With only two girls it is easier to agree, compromises are relatively simple and trust is conferred on just one other person. Communication is simpler and less cluttered; arrangements are easy.

Disadvantages: Being in a pair is great but the more exclusive the paired friendship is the more problematic it can become. For a start, being in a pair means one girl will always be alone when the other has to be away. There are many reasons why one girl might not be there, such as sports fixtures or illness, and different ability sets for various curriculum areas. If a pair of girls operate their friendship largely to the exclusion of other girls it can make them a target. Pairs that appear very strong can generate jealousy, prompting relational aggression from other girls. Girls inside very close pairs can appear to be standoffish and the friendship bond can act as a deterrent to other girls getting to know them. Jealousies can arise; for instance, if one of the pair has a 'maths friend' in her maths set, then the other member of the pair can feel threatened. The strong desire for an exclusive friend can mask some deeper insecurities about trust and friendship.

Some parents may reasonably take the view that spending so much time with just one other girl restricts their daughter's social, emotional and cultural growth. Paired friends that are exclusive don't get to experience a variety of opinions and ways of socialising. In particular, where a parent is not as fond of the close friend as their daughter is, there can be tension. Keeping paired friendship strong but reasonably flexible is the key. Being a genuine best friend means letting your friend spend time with other people without getting anxious or jealous.

Finally, if the pair split up, it can be devastating for the girl who is left entirely on her own. If one girl has behaved unreasonably then the other girl has no one to mediate the behaviour, and no one to facilitate a compromise and reconciliation.

Summary: if your daughter is in an especially close pair it is worth very gently expressing the view that there is more long-term friendship-security to be found in having several friends. It might be wise for her, perhaps with her friend, to spend time with other groups - turning another pair into a four or a three into a five. Your daughter may reject this idea out of hand but there is no harm in sowing the seeds of the thought and letting her process it in her own time. Giving advice is always tricky but giving her a nudge and then stepping back can work well.

Threes

Advantages: With the right personalities, threes can be stable and strong and are probably the most common format. The number in the group is not so large as to create natural splits and the girls very often negotiate their friendships successfully. A group of three is small enough to be intimate and trusting, and yet large enough to provide some variety. In a group of three there is always a 'back up' if one girl is absent, and if two girls fall out then the third can act as a natural facilitator to reconciliation.

Some adults take the view that any friendship group that has an odd number is inherently problematic. However, groups of three are very common and work well. Although schools often require girls to work or sit in pairs, the resulting repeated negotiation to make a group of three successful often empowers them to be consistently aware and considerate of each other's needs.

Disadvantages: Threes can sometimes be tense and stressful because the possibility of being excluded by the other two is always present. When asked, girls will confess that there is often a degree of anxiety when considering whether or not the other two girls in the group are closer to each other than they are to her. Any shared interest between two of them can feel like a threat to the third.

Many of the seating arrangements in society are organised in pairs. The desks in school and the minibuses - seats are so often arranged two-by-two! Though mentioned above as an advantage, teachers can nonetheless be guilty of causing real agony with the simple instruction, 'In pairs, please discuss the following topic.'

If two girls in a group of three fall out with each other it can leave the third girl in a very awkward position. The third girl may have to work hard not to take sides whilst also trying to affect some sort of resolution to the argument.

Summary: If your daughter's group of three is not going well then don't just assume that that is because there are an odd number of girls in the group. When you have three girls who get on with each other, the group-of-three can be very successful. Taking seriously the girls' need to operate as a three rather than a pair will likely feel validating and empower them to strengthen their friendships.

Fours

Advantages: Fours can be split into two pairs and pairs, as we have seen, are a naturally strong format. We have also seen how school desks and buses often have pairs of seats, and that suits the group of four as well.

The more girls there are in a group then the more invitations to parties and gatherings there are; variety and fluidity are increased, leading to richer social engagement.

There is also safety in numbers; each individual girl is unlikely ever to be on their own when there are three others in the group.

Disadvantages: With higher numbers in a group comes a degree of inflexibility. If the group wants to engage in a social activity on a Saturday afternoon and one girl cannot make it, do they go? This is a question that generates much debate amongst girls. While the absence of one girl is not reason enough to cancel a trip, the very least we might expect is that the feelings of the one left behind are respected. That might mean a constant flow of social media pictures, videos and comments to make the left-behind-girl feel included. Or it might mean the opposite - it might protect her feelings more if there was a social media blackout around the event. Deciding how to cope with these scenarios is something to be negotiated between the girls, and the very fact that negotiation is taking place is good and helpful in preventing hurt and fallouts.

The larger the group the more likely the girls are to see themselves as a little gang or clique and this can be unhelpful for the rest of the girls around them. Cliques can create a sense of being 'in' or 'out' - 'cool' or 'not cool'. Furthermore, as girls mature and their personalities change it can put a strain on the clannish identities of these larger groups. This means that when the time comes for a clique to change its identity, tensions and arguments can arise leading to painful break-ups of friendships. For example, if part of the group identity is a shared admiration for a particular pop singer, it can be difficult when some girls decide their tastes have changed - perhaps becoming more alternative or 'edgy'. It can be especially hard for parents if the new 'identity' of the group is based around something like vaping, where those girls who disapprove are then deemed to be excluding themselves from the clique. The longer the history of the clique, the more painful the end of those friendships can be.

Summary: if your daughter is in a happy group of four and those girls also move in and out of other groups too, then all is well. If the group tends to be exclusive then you need to watch out for the time when things change and the common interests they shared no longer act as a bond in their friendships. Encouraging fluidity between groups is always good but don't expect your advice to be especially welcomed or acted upon straight away.

More than Four

Groups of more than four spring up from time to time and are common in bigger schools. They are often characterised by smaller subgroups existing within a bigger whole.

Advantages: The 'clumping' effect of subgroups to create a larger group can be beneficial because it can aid positive fluidity. Many girls openly welcome the opportunity to move between friendship groups in a way that feels secure and trusting. The mere presence of these larger groups, and the fluidity they encourage can have a positive influence on the way all friendships are framed in that year group.

Disadvantages: Larger groups can be unwieldy and cumbersome. If big groups form around specific identities, such as girls who are good at sport, or girls who like a particular style of music, tensions can arise between groups. It can be particularly uncomfortable if the group identity is based on ethnicity.

Summary: if your daughter reports that she is in a group of more than five then expect there to be subgroups within that. The movement of friends within those subgroups may be working well or it may cause one or two girls within the bigger group to be left out from time to time as friendship configurations change.

Inter-group conflict

It is not uncommon for there to be conflict between groups of friends in school. Sometimes a group of girls will bond over their decision to show disrespect to another group. They find themselves using condemnatory language about the other group who inevitably find out and inter-group conflict ensues. Although this conflict may appear to have a specific agenda – an incident that occurred on the playground or at a sleepover, or a perceived slight in a text conversation – at the root will be the search for trusting and reliable friendships. It is unfortunate that girls sometimes bond over plotting claims and counterclaims against other friendship groups, but it is a reality in many schools. As a parent you should listen to and monitor what you are being told and be prepared to talk to the school if things are getting out of hand.

Blending

While thinking about group sizes, it is important to bear in mind that school-age children often feel a significant pressure to blend in with their peers and be accepted by their peer group. This is certainly not unique to girls; to some extent all human beings seek to blend with each other and with the shared identity of their group. Blending does not mean simply mimicking everything everyone else does; girls expect each other to have separate tastes and identities but also to have enough in common to form a bond.

A degree of blending with each other enables girls to find common ground on which to form friendships. A girl who makes active choices to be obviously different from her friends across a whole range of aspects of her identity - humour, sports, clothes, music and so on - presents tension for her friends. As we have seen, the development of a girl's identity is often tightly bound with friendships. This can explain why making different choices can feel challenging and unsettling for a friendship group: if one girl chooses a different path, what does that say about the choices the others have made? There is a balance to be struck between celebrating uniqueness (being true to yourself and enhancing your self-worth) and prioritising finding things in common with others.

That is why it can be so hard to put forward new and different ideas, to be the first to try new identities and choose to be different. It generally becomes easier and more comfortable in late adolescence and adulthood to celebrate differences between ourselves and others, but for school-age children the pressure to blend can be strong.

However, whilst some of the things that makes a girl different from her friends are the result of active choices she has made, other aspects of difference may be beyond her control. For example, a girl's ethnic, religious or cultural background can make her different to her peers, as can her gender identity and sexual orientation. Being neuro-atypical, or having special educational needs or a disability can also be a source of difference. For all these types of differences, parents need to support their daughters with additional understanding that it can be problematic to be under pressure to blend in with dominant norms.

"Just be yourself"

There are many books, videos, blogs, vlogs and assorted messages on multiple platforms that are aimed at encouraging girls and young women to be individually empowered. Authors like Laura Bates do a great job in de-mystifying the process of growing up for adolescents and seek also to encourage the individual to be themselves. We undertook a piece of Facebook and Twitter research, in which people (both genders) were asked what advice they would give their 13-year-old selves. The answers from women were surprisingly uniform and included statements such as: "Just be yourself', "It's Okay not always to fit in", "Wear those trainers if that is what you want to do", 'Don't feel you have to spend all your time with just two other girls".

What the answers shared was a sense that, once they had reached adulthood, the respondents looked back at the struggles of childhood and adolescence and saw that the need to blend limited their freedoms. Now mature and more confident in their identity, they regretted that they had felt such an urgent need to be accepted by their peers. Perhaps what the respondents had forgotten was the intensity of their need to blend in at that earlier stage of their development.

The need to blend felt by nearly all girls in school far outweighs the call, from adults, to be individual and proudly different. The encouragement by adults to 'just be yourself' is yet one more source of frustration and pressure for girls. How girls create and project their identity in order to blend and be accepted is complex. Projecting the wrong image of herself is, as in the words of Regina George from the movie *Mean Girls*, tantamount to 'social suicide'.

CHAPTER THREE

Types of Behaviour and Experiences

Coming up in this chapter:
"...every girl looking to create friendship bonds needs to work on finding things she might have in common with another girl."

In this chapter we look at what happens on the ground; what is it like to be a girl in school, navigating the choppy waters of friendship? We will describe some typical ways in which girls behave in order to provide both girls and adults with the language to understand how and why friendships work. It is important to establish, though, that what follows here are descriptions of experiences and behaviours, and not personalities. Why girls take on particular roles in groups is likely to be the result of group dynamics that are inherently impossible to predict. Many parents describe that their daughter's experience of friendship is markedly different at school compared with when she is at an extracurricular club or other group situation. The roles and behaviours girls adopt become defined in relation to each other and the wider group. We do not seek to pass judgement or pigeon-hole individuals, especially at this fluid period of development. These are strictly descriptions of types of experiences and behaviour - not girls.

Girl-in-the-water

A Girl-in-the-water is a girl who has no friendship group, either because she is a New Girl - new to her school and so has no friends; or she is a Casualty Girl - a girl who has been removed from, or has left her group and has no apparent in-school friendships. A Girl-in-the-water is likely to be experiencing relationship anxiety. Girls from the wider group will see this and will, at some point, need to make room for her in one of the friendship groups.

The Queen Bee

A girl exhibiting Queen Bee behaviour will exert power over other girls which is not always wanted or appropriate. She may quickly form very close bonds with one girl for a week or two and then, equally as suddenly, she will pull away and move on to someone else. Queen Bee behaviour is characterised by manipulation of both peers and adults in an attempt to ensure the pool of possible friendships never runs dry; it's about staying in complete control. In this context, the term manipulation is used to describe the outward effect when a girl is working in the zone of breaking implicit but not explicit rules, described in Chapter 2. Girls adopt Queen Bee behaviour often as a result of being especially insecure about their friendships, or anxious about their ability to form bonds. Through attempts to both control and disrupt social interactions, they manage their own anxieties about how to build secure friendships.

'Queen Bee' is a pejorative term and no girl likes to be accused of this form of behaviour. It can be hard for parents to accept that their daughter exhibits Queen Bee behaviour and holding her directly to account can cause upset and disconnection. However, more positive forms of behaviour can be encouraged by helping her to see that Queen Bee behaviour, in the long run, undermines the closeness between her and her friends and therefore perpetuates rather than lessens feelings of insecurity. Simply inviting her to reflect that her behaviour might be described as 'Queen Bee' can often be the start of her journey to become more secure and self-reliant.

Queen Bee behaviour can have a strong negative influence on an entire cohort of girls in a school. Because of the dominant nature of this kind of behaviour it can be hard for other, more community-enhancing forms of behaviour to surface.

Leaders

In life we see people who seem to have natural charisma, and leadership comes to them often without them even seeking the role. When we see leadership behaviour in school-aged girls which is positive and selfless we should applaud it wholeheartedly. It is not easy to show leadership within girl cohorts at school because behaviour that is seen to depart from the norm can so easily be rejected. Leadership is often just about saying, 'Hey, let's do this instead of that.' But it only takes a few side-glances for the idea to be quickly rejected by the other girls. Feeling that you are not accepted within the group then causes pain and the decision to refrain from leadership behaviour in the future soon follows.

Leadership behaviour can be deliberately misinterpreted and criticised by other girls as being 'bossy' or controlling. This is a shame given that leadership is such a vital and empowering form of behaviour and can help an entire cohort to be happy. It takes real strength of character to show leadership as a girl in school. Schools that are truly aspirational in their support of girls' life outcomes tend to produce many more girls who are comfortable identifying as leaders.

Parental support of leadership behaviour is hard because it has to be acknowledged that the pressure to be accepted far outweighs the desire to rise above the crowd. If a parent finds themselves frustrated by their daughter's perceived inability to 'stand up' within the group, then they need to appreciate the conflicting pressures involved in this role.

Strategies to build the confidence to lead should be subtle, positive and focused on the idea that leadership can be used to secure stronger friendships. Parents should encourage daughters to take the lead in order to create stronger friendships. Parents can also support leadership moments by being there to take the blame if an idea is rejected and being recessive if an idea is successful. For example:

Daughter: My parent says it would be great to go to the Burger place on the High Street on Saturday.

If that idea is accepted then she gets the credit; if it is rejected, she can blame the parent!

Would-be Leaders

Sometimes girls try to assert themselves over other girls in order to try to gain control but, for whatever reason, their attempts fail. Their efforts can even backfire and make them less popular. Girls exhibiting 'would-be leader' behaviour can become frustrated because they seem to lack the natural ability to lead or influence other girls and cannot understand why their suggestions are undermined. They can become envious of those girls who demonstrate leadership quality, and that envy can undermine their own sense of identity.

A girl whose attempts at leadership are rejected may feel humiliated and decide not to lead again. What is different about would-be leaders is that they feel frustration rather than humiliation and so they keep trying.

Supporting a girl to move away from this form of behaviour involves strategies that make her feel empowered and secure in other ways. However, parents must avoid the trap of feeling indignant on behalf of their daughter. Validating her frustration is important, but it is also key to move beyond vengeful feelings and promote problem-solving. Encourage her to lead by example, to influence the influencers, to be present and willing at all times. Show her that having been unsuccessful in her leadership attempt is not a personal weakness, that 'going along' with the others is not a failure and that negotiation and compromise are important skills too.

The Peacemaker

Girls who exhibit Peacemaker behaviour often do so time and again.

The Peacemaker is a girl who just wants everyone to get on. She can be popular and sought after as a Best Friend because she is easy-going and does not cause conflict. Her aim is to smooth over potential trouble and find ways to compromise so that everyone is included and happy. Peacemakers can be very adept at navigating a smooth passage between warring factions without losing face or damaging their integrity. Some girls can accuse the Peacemaker of being two-faced because she appears to agree with opposite opinions. Some adults involved may feel this is a weak position for a girl to take because it appears passive and unassertive. Equally, it can be argued that this behaviour is to be much applauded because without such girls there would be much more conflict and friendship turbulence. To be a successful Peacemaker takes courage and skill.

However, being a Peacemaker can lead to some awkward situations because it is not always possible to support both sides of an argument. Sometimes the Peacemaker can become weary of always being the one to find compromises. The compromises she negotiates might make her feel like she is never the one to get her own way. It can be useful, therefore, to encourage the Peacemaker to make her own feelings felt and be assertive of her own right to happiness. For parents, a starting point may be simply helping her to explore what it would look and feel like if she had her own needs met. As much as anything, the Peacemaker is entitled to take credit as the peacemaker.

The Hopper

Like the Peacemaker, girls who display Hopper behaviour often do so consistently.

A Hopper has legitimate membership of many friendship groups and can 'hop' from one to another without causing upset or jealousy. However, many girls find they are unable to be Hoppers; for some it works well and for others the group dynamics mean it is an impossibility. Hoppers have the ability to blend with a wide variety of groups, fit in and be liked.

Inherent to Hopper behaviour is a belief that the whole point of school is for everyone to be friends with everyone else. These girls are often seen to prioritise befriending everyone in the class, almost systematically. They naturally prefer to have a whole-class birthday party, they are curious about their peers and keen to integrate newcomers. They expertly conform to the implicit friendship rules and are keen to ease tensions. They gently resist girls who seek to involve them in exclusive friendships.

Parents may wish to promote this attitude by encouraging their daughters to make friends with **everyone**. Parents of older girls can check in with their daughters by opening conversations about all the girls in their class and encourage her to form connections. Parents of younger girls can help in practical ways, such as organising different playdates or facilitating whole-class parties.

As girls grow into adulthood they tend to become more comfortable with Hopper-like behaviour, so we might conclude that Hoppers are more mature and confident than their peers. A cohort of girls that has several Hoppers in it can often be a very happy year group. Where Hoppers set the tone and dominate the culture of how friendships are operated, there is less jealousy and less conflict. Hoppers often also look after Girls-in-the-water.

The Messenger

Messenger behaviour is when a girl relays secrets between groups in order to strengthen the allegiance between herself and the other girls. This strategy can be successful in the short term but goes badly wrong when other girls find out their 'private' conversations have been leaked to others. This is a form of behaviour which is widely recognised by girls and widely disapproved of too.

Lonely Girl

Lonely Girl describes the experience and/or behaviour of a girl who seems unable to find consistent and stable friendships, though explicitly not as a result of bullying, which is discussed below. Rather this describes a girl who feels she can't develop a persistent bond with others and there can be many reasons for this.

It might be that the girl was badly hurt by friendship issues that went wrong for her in the past - she may have even been ill-treated and is struggling now to learn to trust other girls. She needs time, gentleness and compassion to recover and learn to trust again.

It might be that a girl has this experience because her approach to friendship is working against the grain of the wider habits of the group, so that her attempts to befriend don't fall into place. She may find herself persistently at odds with the implicit friendship rules at play, for example because she finds them confusing, alienating or silly. She may feel out of place because of other past experiences, life circumstances or demographic factors. She may also feel that she badly wants a friend, but that her independence of character is compromised by attempts at integration. This is a conflict she needs to be helped to resolve.

Whether caused by approach or circumstances, a girl can be supported through a Lonely Girl experience in a variety of ways. First of all, it needs to be acknowledged by all (not least the girl herself) that this situation is a result of many factors, and not a reflection of her fundamental ability to be and have a friend. Secondly, she needs to be helped to engage and engage wholeheartedly. In other words, every girl looking to create friendship bonds needs to work on finding ways to prioritise relating and empathising with the others. This might start with finding things she has in common with another girl. This can take time and effort and it is important to keep trying.

It is possible for any girl to find herself in this situation given the right unfortunate circumstances. However, it can be fruitful to ask what other factors are pushing a Lonely Girl into this position. The answers to this are multifarious and unique to individuals. Sometimes a girl's relationship with her parent has not evolved and matured as quickly as her peers' relationships with their parents. Perhaps she has become over-reliant on her parent for emotional support at the expense of seeking closeness with other girls. As a consequence she does not feel the Existential Imperative (every girl needs a friend) as keenly as other girls because, in effect, her parent is her friend. Strategies to encourage self-confidence should be explored. Let her find herself through the choices she makes.

When people are friends it is nearly always because they have shared experiences. It is therefore important for the girls to find things they have in common. This could be achieved by creating shared experiences such as going out to the cinema together, a trip to a bowling alley, or a meal in a cafe. Equally important are smaller shared moments, such as remembering a joke or finding minor commonalities (e.g. we both have annoying younger brothers). Anything that provides experiences which are unique to the group will help with the bonding process. Those experiences can be facilitated by a parent but equally the parent should be careful to encourage independence and self-reliance; the experience is something to be shared amongst the peer group and not so much with the parent.

Lonely Girl experiences are not uncommon and can cause a lot of distress for all concerned. The simple strategies listed above can be very effective and it is important to stay calm and give it time.

The Singleton

As distinct from Lonely Girl behaviour the Singleton is a girl for whom the whole idea of the Existential Imperative does not seem to matter. She is happy and content in her own company, though she will often have friends too. If her friends show relational aggression towards her, she just ignores it. This is not a category of girl behaviour that parents can guide their daughter towards. The Singleton just seems to possess the ability to remain slightly disconnected from all the girls around her; this is both a strength and a burden since what she gains in avoiding friendship turbulence and not being prey to the Existential Imperative she sometimes loses in the absolute closeness of good friendships.

The Bully

The Bully is a rare thing. Often driven by deep-seated jealousy and insecurity, the Bully stands accused of relational aggression that 'crosses the line'. By this we mean that adult observers can clearly identify forms of behaviour that fulfil the criteria of bullying: a sustained attempt to make a child feel put down and uncomfortable. No girl wants to be a bully or thought of as mean and when they are shown the effect of their behaviour on others they often make the necessary adjustments. These adjustments come about partly because they are driven by adult authority which carries the threat of sanctions, but also because the Bully will quickly realise that once she is exposed as a Bully she will lose friends and therefore the Existential Imperative kicks in.

We look in more detail at this unfortunate aspect of human interaction in Appendix 1.

Conclusion

In this chapter we have presented vocabulary and shared ways to look at girls' behaviour within friendships. This will be useful when, in the next chapter, we look at communication and how to overcome the barriers that often exist between generations.

CHAPTER FOUR

Getting communication right - the barriers caused by generational disconnect

Coming up in this chapter:
"Please just listen. This is my life right now. I am not telling you because you need to know but because I need to tell you."

It is part of the human condition that every generation considers itself to be new and different. Young adults are usually reluctant to take too much guidance and advice from the older generation because they feel they are going to bring a fresh and revolutionary perspective to everything in the world! Meanwhile, by the time we reach adulthood, we have often forgotten the intricacies and agonies of teenage emotions, anxieties and group dynamics.

Communication between generations can be challenging, and teen and pre-teen girls talking to their parents are no exception. Times move on, new trends become cool, and different blunders become embarrassing. Girls often struggle to communicate these troubles to parents, and parents in turn fail to recall how central they are to young girls.

This deficiency in shared vocabulary, experience and emotion leads to a communication difficulty that we call **generational disconnect**. When sons and parents disconnect we might see sons become mute and resort to grunting their responses.

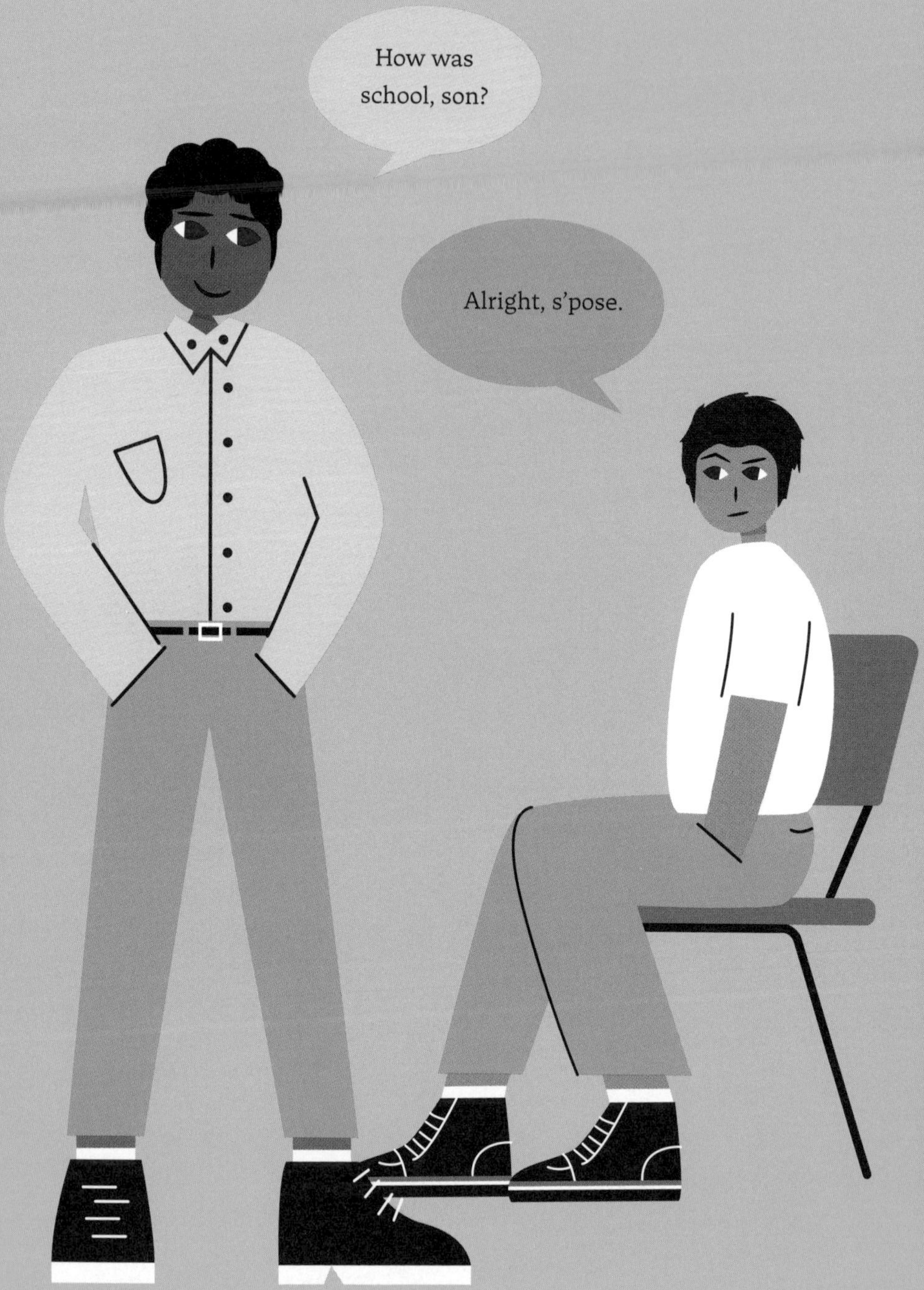
How was school, son?
Alright, s'pose.

When daughters and parents disconnect it can be harder to spot.

At the heart of the problem is the fact that what is said and what is heard are not the same thing.

Your teachers say that you *can* work harder. I want you to be the best you can be in your school work - give it all you've got and I know you can achieve great things!

Daughter hears: You're saying that I won't do well unless I work really hard. If I was clever I wouldn't need to work hard, so you must think I am *stupid*.

Another example, this time the other way round.

These shoes you make me wear for school are just horrible and everyone is laughing at me because of them.

Parent hears: You are upset because this is a new school year and you haven't settled in yet.

What is being said

When a girl tells her story after a day of friendship turbulence it is a moment of catharsis and emotional release. She is telling her parent about her experiences, about what happened from her point of view and why, right now, she is upset. Her story is one of a litany of stories told every day by every girl across the globe and they all tell the same tale. It is not a narrative of wrongdoing! It is instead simply another iteration of how the Existential Imperative (every girl needs a friend) plays out in her life. She is telling her parent how important it is to have a friend and how seemingly impossible it feels, at that moment, to find trusting and reliable friendships. Nothing more, nothing less. As she tells her story to her parent, she thinks,

'Please just listen. This is my life right now. I am not telling you because you need to know but because I need to tell you.

*I need to tell **someone** the story of my day, and right now I am doing you the honour of telling you - just you.*

Don't spoil it.'

What is heard

Because the story often includes conflict which has upset a daughter and/or others, a parent will interpret the story as a tale of wrongdoing. As a consequence, the parent feels the need to probe for clarification, perhaps by asking a series of closed questions. The parent may make assumptions based on their own judgements. The parent then sees their role as 'rescuer' or 'wise adjudicator'. From this position the parent will dispense unwanted wisdom and possibly start to take action - looking to attribute blame.

The parent has missed the point. This probing and problem-solving will be felt as judgmental by the daughter. The position of blame-seeking will feel at best alienating and at worst threatening to the girl, who is in fact just trying to process a complex social interaction. It does not take many repetitions of this misunderstanding for the girl to resolve not to say anything of any real importance about friendships to her parent ever again. If stories of friendship turbulence are always greeted by advice (makes her feel patronised), probing questions (makes her feel judged), or solutions (makes her incredulous) then, unsurprisingly, a daughter will seek other audiences for her outpourings.

'Mum/Dad, I am going to my room and I shall see you when I am 18. If I need anything you'll be the first to know.'

Focus on the emotion

Focusing too much on the detail of the girl's convoluted story can leave both parent and daughter confused and misdirected. Instead, it is more helpful to focus on the emotional content of what is being said. Is the girl expressing frustration? Despair? Low confidence? Parents can use open questions to gain a deeper understanding; (e.g. 'How did you feel about that?'), paving the way for a more validating and supportive conversation; (e.g. 'That must have been very hard for you.'). This is explored further in Chapter 7.

It is not uncommon for girls to turn to the family dog as their favoured confidante, because the dog doesn't judge, offer advice, ring the school, ring the other parent, write aggressive emails, patronise, judge.

Two elements of communication

It is useful to divide communication coming from a daughter into two elements: the words and the emotional subtext.

1. The **words** she is saying will often involve a complex narrative. There may be exaggeration and dramatisation.
2. Just below the surface of the words is the **emotional subtext**. She will reveal the truth about her feelings through the hyperbole and drama, through the condemnation and disgust.

In order to support a daughter in the most effective way, a parent must understand *why* the story is being told. The emotional sub-text is far more important than the meaning of the actual words spoken. She wants to say that she had a bad day and she is feeling a range of powerful and challenging emotions which she would like help with. She wants comfort and reassurance, and she wants the chance to try to articulate her feelings through words. The trouble comes when the events that triggered those feelings seem just too trivial and nuanced to the parent, to cross the threshold of credibility. So she exaggerates, or as some adults say, she '**makes a drama**' out of her distress.

For example, a girl may complain about another girl staring at her. This is making her feel uncomfortable and as though the girl staring is sending hate towards her. Usually, a teacher or parent would be reluctant to start taking action against someone because of the way another person looked at them - it doesn't cross the threshold of seriousness. The adult's instinct might be to say, 'oh just ignore them'. So, in order to get the adult's attention, the girl will exaggerate her distress, and the story she tells will become more 'dramatic' in order to cross the threshold.

We can see that making a 'drama' out of things is a girl's attempt to illustrate the emotional intensity of her response to an event. Let's be careful not to condemn girls employing this tactic. Let's replace the phrase 'attention seeking' with 'attention needing.'

I just had the worst day anyone could ever have, ever!

That's terrible - what on earth happened?"

Debbie told Sandra that she didn't like my hair band. And it's your fault!"

'Adapted truth'

Girls will tell an adapted version of the truth in order to trigger the response from the parent she needs. The trouble is that the adult, understandably, does not hear that but accepts the tale at face value. The adult will hear the story and scrutinise it for wrongdoing before then dispensing 'wise advice'.

When a daughter starts to tell the story of her day, a parent should always say to themselves:

"What I am about to hear is probably the adapted truth. It is adapted in order to show how she really feels and to get a particular reaction from me which I must be careful to understand and get right. I must be careful not to get lost in the detail or be judgmental of her or others. What she probably needs from me is a gentle and subtle acknowledgment of the emotion she is experiencing. And that's all."

Conclusion

This chapter has been about generational disconnect and what causes it. It usually stems from a simple but fundamental misunderstanding of what is being said and what is being heard. To learn how to bridge the divide between the generations, we need to hear the voice of the young person louder and more clearly. A girl can find it hard to use that voice at home because she:

- Doesn't want to appear rude, ungrateful, cheeky or unloving
- Doesn't yet know how to find the right words to say what she feels
- Doesn't yet know that feeding back her constructive criticism of your parenting would make a difference. She assumes your parenting style is immoveable.

Chapter 5 looks in more detail at the reasons why girls lie to their parents and gives some detailed examples.

Telling parents the truth

Coming up in this chapter:
"We all have to manipulate from time to time, often for the best of reasons."

We all regard truth, honesty and integrity as key components of a civilised society. Equally, we know that the occasional 'white lie' is needed to avoid giving offence, keep social interactions sweet and functioning, or even to avoid discovery of a minor misdeed.

- A friend buys an expensive coat and asks for your opinion.
- A young child presents you with a cup of tea made with water from the hot tap.
- A work colleague asks who took the last biscuit.

These are all situations in which we may find ourselves giving answers that are essentially lies. These lies are justified by weighing in the balance any unnecessary conflict and upset that can be avoided with any harm done by the untruth. So, a lie is made up when there is a motivation which is more powerful than the comfort of knowing the truth has been told.

In many cultures, adults openly spin yarns of fairies and monsters, knowing that the child will gradually understand the difference between truth and fallacy. Indeed, the telling of fairy tales is the first way in which we educate children about the multifaceted nature of truth. There comes a point in childhood when parents and/ or teachers will explain the concept of the 'white lie'. However, many children will have already spotted the complexities of this concept long before it is verbalised by an adult.

We underestimate how far children understand the rules governing telling truth and lies. The strategic use of half-truths is actually very common, even in children as young as two. This is, of course, usually easy to spot, (e.g. the toddler with chocolate around her mouth who denies having raided the biscuit tin). At times we actively encourage lying (e.g. "you love Grandma's knitted jumpers don't you?") and can even feel exasperated when our child turns out to be not very good at it ("no, they're ugly and itchy!"). As would be expected, the complexity of the white lies children can execute increases with age.

Research (1) shows that children can start to lie at the age of 2 and that by the age of 4 around 80% have lied in some form. As a girl tells her parent a lie she is simultaneously weighing up the benefits of the lie with the likelihood of the lie being discovered, and what strategies she may be able to employ to distract them and obfuscate if the truth seems about to be revealed. It is useful to use the word 'manipulation' here, despite its negative connotations. We all have to manipulate from time to time, often for the best of reasons. In order to uncover why girls manipulate each other and adults it is essential that parents understand the motivation behind lying.

It is generally uncomfortable to discover we have been lied to in any situation, even if we can recognise this was done to save our feelings. We may feel embarrassed, angry or excluded by the dishonesty. When a parent discovers their child has lied, these responses are heightened by a sense of loss of control. A parent can feel as if they have lost full insight into their child's life, despite feeling responsible for their actions. This can lead to anger at the disloyalty or anxiety at not knowing what is really going on. A parent may feel very hurt by what feels like a loss of honesty or connection. So being lied to can provoke powerful responses in parents. Ironically it is these powerful reactions which can sometimes fuel the very reasons the lie was made in the first place. What can get lost is understanding the subtlety and nuance behind what motivates us all to lie.

Reasons to lie

Here we examine a number of scenarios which lead a girl to make the decision to lie. In doing so, we illustrate how complex these social interactions can be. While reading these examples, it is helpful to have in mind how a punishing response to lying can lead the parent or teacher to miss the real issues at play.

A girl may lie because she does not want to get told off or punished by her parent. She may disguise or twist the truth in order to ensure her story is interpreted in the way she feels is necessary.

59

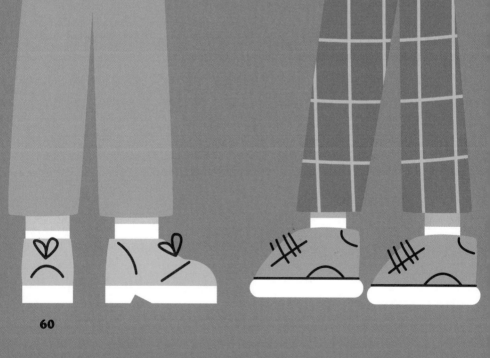

61

A girl may lie to avoid her parent focussing on the wrong narrative detail.
Amy is obviously upset after school. Her mum encourages her to confide in her about what's been happening. Amy says she is upset because she hasn't been invited to Bella's sleepover at the weekend. She neglects to tell her mum that in fact Bella had asked her last week, before the other girls. However, Amy had turned down the offer as she thought the rest of her friendship group might make other plans.

Amy knows her Mum takes great pride in how thoughtful Amy is to others. She holds strong moral values on honesty and kindness. Amy also knows that if her Mum detects any evidence of wrongdoing, she will likely focus unduly on that, neglecting to understand the wider context of the story or acknowledge the wrongdoing of others. In order to avoid this misdirection, Amy lies.

A girl may lie because friendship turbulence can be embarrassing and difficult to express precisely.

Hey, let's go to the mall after school. Luke is going and I really like him.

Amaya thinks: Oh dear, Vicki is my best friend but I haven't told her that I have been texting Luke all week now.

I don't know, I need to finish my homework first...

...I asked Luke if he wanted to hang out in town on Saturday but he told me he only wanted to come if you are going because he knows you like him. You're the worst best friend ever!

A girl may lie because situations governing the moment-by-moment status of a friendship can be very fluid and very hard to communicate.

Serena, Molly and Anju have only just become friends, having arrived at their secondary school only a few days earlier. While their friendship is still new, tender and fragile they find themselves falling out over small things - like whether Anju's school bag is cooler than Molly's or whether Serena's older brother is clever or not. Their conversations are attempting to be ironic and witty but they are struggling with the boundary between irony and unintentional insult. They frequently stray into areas they find hard to control and feelings get hurt.

All three girls are upset when they go home. Their upset is as much based on confusion and disappointment as any real sense of slight. Even as she is trying to explain to her parent why she is upset, Anju receives messages on a group text platform from Serena full of apology and regret. Anju sees the three flashing dots on her phone screen that indicate that Molly is writing a reply. Because she is upset and looking at her phone, Anju's parent takes it away and decides to keep it until the morning to 'give her a break'. Anju is in agony, desperate to know what Molly has replied. However, explaining what is happening is impossible - she doesn't really know what's happening because it is entirely fluid at that moment. To get back her phone Anju makes up a story about how mean her maths teacher was to her in class and how he had set her extra homework. The only way she can access the work is from her phone...

A girl may lie to honour the intensity and closeness of their friendships (I): backing up a friend and their lie.

15-year-old Anne is in an abusive relationship with a 17-year-old boy who attends the 6th form at her school. She confides in her best friend Isobel and swears her to secrecy. As the abuse gets worse Anne finds she can no longer go to school without having panic attacks. She tells her parent that she is experiencing bad period pains to excuse her attendance at school. Only Isobel knows the truth. When Anne's mother starts to piece together an accurate understanding of the situation having seen text messages on Anne's phone, she asks Isobel if she knows what is really going on. Isobel denies all knowledge of the boy and repeats the lie about period pains.

A girl may lie to honour the intensity and closeness of their friendships (II): seeking revenge and settling old scores.

When Amelia, Charlotte and Jenna were 11, Amelia was always rather over-dominant. She played with her friends' feelings at times and Charlotte and Jenna felt manipulated and controlled. But they were too young to understand how to protect themselves and how to out-smart Amelia. Now that the girls are 14, things have changed. Charlotte and Jenna have a much clearer understanding of how Amelia gets her own way and over the summer they make a pact that they are no longer going to let Amelia control them.

Within a week of the beginning of term, there is tension as Amelia starts to orchestrate ways to separate Charlotte and Jenna. Amelia feeds both Charlotte and Jenna little secrets to test their loyalty to her. However, after their summer pact, Charlotte and Jenna secretly confide in each other about Amelia's manipulation. They decide to spread rumours about Amelia and boys - making out that Amelia has loose morals and telling stories that have apparent credibility and are hard to disprove. Amelia tells her parents who complain to the school. The Head of Year interviews Jenna and Charlotte separately and asks each for the truth about these rumours. They both deny any knowledge and the Head of Year accepts this as they've always been good girls in the past. Without explicitly realising it, the Head of Year has effectively asked both Jenna and Charlotte to choose between truth and loyalty to their friend (the existential imperative).

A girl may lie to honour the intensity and closeness of their friendships (III): building credit and securing loyalty .

Maddy is accused of cheating in a Maths test by her teacher who had inadvertently left the answers to the test on Maddy's desk. Maddy's desk partner, Tilly, seizes her chance to build credit with Maddy. Tilly lies to the teacher that she had indeed left the answers on their desk but the page had been turned over and the answers were not visible. Tilly chooses to lie because the benefit of building closeness to Maddy outweighs the possible punishment.

A girl may lie because she wishes to create turbulence amongst a group of girls. She hopes that friendships will have to be reconfigured which may benefit her. This is the disrupter approach.

Amy has never felt entirely secure in her friendship group with Emma and Remmie. The wider group of friends get on well and there is a good degree of healthy fluidity amongst several groups, adding up to around a dozen girls. Amy can't rid herself of the feeling that she is bottom of the friendship hierarchy and that other friendship groups are more fun and have higher status than hers. Almost on the spur of the moment, Amy sends out a series of texts one evening. Some are to groups, others to individuals. The texts are random bits of gossip, some supportive, some aggressive. She includes some boys in her campaign and they soon respond and stir up more trouble. By the time she arrives in school the next day relations are in turmoil. Friends are arguing, boys are getting involved. Amy plays the victim and waits for her chance to form new and fresh allegiances.

Responding to lies: getting drawn into the quicksand of right and wrong

When a girl tells a story of upset and friendship issues at school, many parents are keen to examine every aspect of the story to try to 'get to the bottom of it'. If a lie is detected amongst the complex fabric of the narrative, a parent will often focus heavily on this aspect. It is not uncommon for a parent to operate this moral filter even to the exclusion of the broader picture or acknowledging the wrongdoing of others. They may say 'I don't care what the others have done, I care that you lied to me!'. To the parent in this moment, it is the lie that feels most important. As we have seen, to the girl this is very unlikely to be the case.

In adopting this stance, a parent encounters two dangers. Firstly, by admonishing their daughter, a parent has made a judgment about where the truth resides in the story. The truth is hard to be certain of and treating all lies with a telling-off undermines what we know about the complex motives behind this universal human behaviour. This leads to the second danger: the daughter will feel that the act of sharing a difficult moment at school has simply resulted in disapproval. The daughter will be reluctant to share her troubles again, or at the very least she will make sure the stories she tells in the future never show her in a bad light.

Conclusion

It is always uncomfortable to think that daughters lie to their parents, but the truth this chapter has sought to reveal is that those lies are understandable when seen from her point of view. That doesn't make lying right or any less painful to receive, but it does give us a better understanding of the questions we need to ask to uncover what is really going on for her. In the next chapter we look in more detail at what can happen at school to make a girl upset.

1. Evans and Lee: Developmental Psychology 2013

CHAPTER SIX

Why girls get upset and why adult intervention can make things worse

Coming up in this chapter:

"...unhappiness will have its roots in the existential imperative: she needs and is always seeking reliable and trusting friendships."

In this chapter we analyse what might be happening in the mind of a typical girl when she feels that things are going wrong with her friendships. We will see that, with the best intentions, adults' attempts to intervene can amplify problems in these fragile and fluid situations. Let's look at a girl called Femi, and examine what happens when she complains that she is unhappy with her friends.

Unless she is being bullied, the reason for friendship-related unhappiness will have its roots in the Existential Imperative: she needs and is always seeking reliable and trusting friendships and that search can be tough and uncertain. She is unhappy because she senses that her friends are growing apart from her or she worries that new bonds are being formed between other girls that do not include her.

Here are some typical things that might be happening in Femi's mind that are causing her to feel unhappy. Each one might be an accurate perception of her friendships. Equally they may be misperceptions, situations viewed through the filter of worry or self-doubt.

Femi may complain to an adult that she is unhappy because:

- she went to the toilet and when she came back her friends had all left the room;
- when she entered a classroom she thought her friends all giggled, and looked at each other;
- her friends all agreed they liked white shoes, but when she bought some, they seemed to laugh at her;
- she wonders what her friends talk about when she is not there;
- all her friends want to play football at breaktime but she has never got the hang of it;
- her friends are all in the bottom Maths set but she is in the top set;
- her friends all want to go to see a local rock band but her parent won't let her go;
- all her friends have pets and she does not;
- all her friends walk to school together but she lives too far away and has to come by bus.

All these situations make her feel under-confident about her friendships and left out.

We could list many more worry-inducing incidents and that girls commonly talk about with adults. Femi may find that just talking things through with an adult is enough and her fears are soothed, particularly if the adult gives due attention to her emotions. But she may find that a reassuring chat is not enough and her worries and unhappiness persist.

White Shoes

Let's take the example of the white shoes: Femi says she is upset because her friends laughed at her white shoes. Her seemingly straightforward complaint is potentially very complex, with many hidden variables. We know that Femi is anxious about her friendships and she may well be using the white shoes incident to encapsulate her concern. Her anxiety may be causing her to over-interpret looks, gestures and situations negatively.

In order to force the teacher to take her upset seriously Femi may exaggerate her complaint and claim that her friends are being mean to her. As illustrated in Chapter 5, she may distort the truth strategically to reach her goal of getting the adult to see her point of view.

At this point Femi's complaint would be dealt with by a teacher with sympathetic listening, an investigation to find the truth and possible consequences to deliver justice. But uncovering the actual truth is far from simple. Let's take just two possible ways in which this scenario might play out.

Maybe:
It is possible that Femi's friends were indeed being mean to her about her shoes. They may have all agreed to say they loved white shoes but were playing a trick on Femi. They knew she would go and buy white shoes if they all said they liked them and that would give them the chance to laugh at her when they saw her wearing them. In this scenario wrongdoing has indeed happened and Femi's friends have been mean. However, the task for the adult of uncovering and exposing that meanness is almost impossible – it is too easy for Femi's friends simply to say that they were laughing for joy, not in derision. As long as they all stick to the same story their treachery

will not be discovered. If the teacher, nonetheless, decides to act against Femi's friends and tells them off or punishes them, there is a real chance that those girls will complain to their parents that they have been unfairly treated. The girls know that it is impossible to prove they were being mean and that no adults witnessed the event. By getting their parents to contact the school to complain they can reverse the reprimands. The end result is that the teacher has made the situation worse for Femi and has spent many hours interviewing girls and speaking to their parents in the process. Femi is now further removed from her goal of integration into the friendship group. In short, the teacher's intervention has been a disaster.

Or:

Perhaps, Femi's friends were not being mean to her and were indeed laughing in delight not derision at her new shoes. However, Femi's insecurity and uncertainty over these friendships has reached such a pitch that she feels the need to do something dramatic - something that will make her feel she has some power and influence over her friends. She therefore deliberately misinterprets her friends' laughter knowing full well it was not meant in a mean way. She decides that she has the evidence she needs to complain to an adult and decides to accuse one girl in particular of being the ringleader of meanness. She complains to her parents and they in turn complain to the school demanding that Femi's friends are punished. Keen to deliver justice to a girl who is visibly upset and parents who are assertively angry, the teacher falls right into the trap. She dismisses the protestations of Femi's friends and reprimands them. The situation then unfolds in ways that are similar to the previous scenario. The parents of Femi's friends become equally assertive in their indignation and the teacher ends up in the middle of a storm of conflict and complaint. The school decides that there is serious 'bad blood' now between the girls and moves them around in class to minimise their interaction with each other. Again, Femi is now further removed from her goal of integration into the friendship group.

There are many other ways this scenario could have played out but, whichever way, adult intervention almost invariably makes the situation worse for the girls. Experience also tells us that when this whole inconvenient, time-consuming and complicated operation is finished, the teacher will walk out of her office and see Femi and the girls walking down the corridor arm-in-arm, the best of friends again!

Conclusion

By telling the story of Femi and the white shoes we have built on the previous chapter's exploration of telling the truth to parents. What can appear to be a simple upset can conceal a tangled web of half-truths, insecurity, anxiety, exaggeration and manipulation. Adults can never assume that their interventions will create positive resolutions to friendship turbulence. In the next chapter we look at what daughters really do want from their parent.

CHAPTER SEVEN

What does your daughter want from you?

Coming up in this chapter:
"She needs to know that you understand the complex and sometimes painful emotional landscape she is travelling through and that her feelings are normal and not weird."

Parenting is hard - there is no doubt about that! It is about finding the balance between being loving - showing unconditional and unreserved love; and being exacting - expecting and demanding high standards of moral, ethical and social behaviour, and not forgetting academic engagement.

However, being parented is also hard and this chapter looks at parenting from the point of view of the daughter.

It is easy to overlook the fact that girls have an acute awareness of the parenting they receive compared with their peers. They love their parent unconditionally but equally they can be critical and frank about the quality of the support they receive. Most of all, children want to be heard, acknowledged and endorsed; loving them means listening to their struggles and not always trying to fix them.

They don't need comparisons with siblings or stories of when their parents were young. They don't want solutions or judgments. They want ownership and agency of their own lives and to be allowed to find their own way. They want and need help and support, but for this to be reactive and responsive, not restrictive or controlling. This begins with the toddler wanting to put on their own shoes, to the 17-year-old planning a 'gap' year. They want their parent sitting alongside them – always ready to hear and receive, empower and validate.

When it comes to taking her place amongst her peers, your role is to help your daughter strengthen her friendships by supporting her to build emotional resilience and stamina. Show her that not every upset, cross word or perceived slight is the end of the world and that friendships can grow stronger as a result of adversity. How you support that heightened emotional intelligence in your daughter is something we can now look at in detail.

Age-appropriate parenting
Your daughter wants parenting that is age appropriate. Finding the delicate balance between too much and too little independence is very challenging and so parents may tend to err on the side of caution, regarding their children as less capable than they actually are. There are big shifts during childhood and adolescence which need to be negotiated carefully and perhaps more frequently than you think. This includes things like bedtime, screen time, homework time and alone time. Food can be the source of conflict as well; then there is clothing, bedroom tidiness, the weekly chores, respectful language, being kind to siblings, being helpful, and relationships with wider family. Although your daughter may recognise the importance of these negotiations, nevertheless she will tend to group these things into a single category: Restrictions to Freedom and Independence. The question for a parent is always, how much and when?
When can she:
- go to her first party on her own?
- have her first phone?
- choose her own food?
- buy her own clothes?

Negotiating your daughter's independence is a constant juggling act of empowering her maturity, whilst keeping her safe and protected. Many parents will take the view that she can earn freedom and independence when she has learnt to take responsibility. For example, when she is old enough to tidy her own bedroom, make her own packed lunch, take the vacuum cleaner out of the cupboard and put it away again - then she can have more freedom and independence. This is often a successful approach, though the parent must stick to their side of the bargain by allowing their daughter opportunities to take responsibility.

So, what does she want? She wants you to be on, or slightly ahead of the curve of age-appropriate parenting and never behind it. While a parent may feel that taking a slightly cautious approach is safer and more protective, their daughter is likely to disagree. Being behind that curve means that your parenting will feel patronising and invalidating.

Girls' needs and parents' needs

Maslow's hierarchy-of-need pyramids have often been used to bring clarity and insight to understanding our lives. Maslow argued that human needs could be placed in a hierarchy of importance. The base level and most fundamental need was for physiological wellbeing - in other words food, water and shelter. Above that comes safety, then a sense of love and belonging and so on. His idea was that you cannot move up a level until the one below is satisfied. His original hierarchy was:

Self-actualisation
desire to become the most that one can be

Esteem
respect, self-esteem, status, recognition, strength, freedom

Love and belonging
friendship, intimacy, family, sense of connection

Safety needs
personal security, employment, resources, healthy, property

Physiological needs
air, water, food, shelter, sleep, clothing, reproduction

If we apply the same thinking to the needs of a parent and the needs of a girl, we might find them represented as:

As a **parent**, I need my daughter to be:

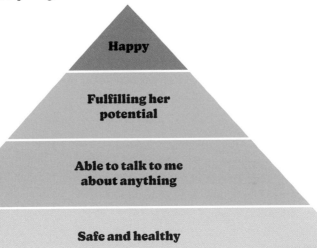

Happy

Fulfilling her potential

Able to talk to me about anything

Safe and healthy

As a **girl**, I need to have:

Autonomy

Access to a non-judgemental listening ear

Access to Social Media

Reliable and trusting friendships

These hierarchies are offered here as a discussion point for parents to reflect on their parenting priorities, rather than a definitive understanding. For instance, some parents might value 'happiness' as more fundamental or might question why 'learning' has not been included. You may feel that girls would want to put 'Safe and Healthy' at their base level – but you could also argue that girls take that for granted and that is why friendships can seem more important to them. What is valuable about this debate is the contrast between the hierarchies of the parent and the daughter. The differences are that parents see their imperatives as providing safety which ultimately leads to happiness and fulfilment; whereas a girl sees her imperatives as social connectedness leading to self-reliance and the ability to 'be herself'.

Seeing life's imperatives from your daughter's point of view will change the way you parent her. The negotiations you engage with and the outcomes you agree to will be more balanced.

Validation

Your daughter wants your validation, and parental validation is crucial to strong mental health. There will be moments when you need to give her unequivocal approval - endorse what she has achieved and praise her attitude and effort. Equally, there will be moments when you need her to reflect on her actions, to correct her attitude and acknowledge that she can do better.

That's fine and she will be prepared to take the praise and the criticism as long as it is fair. She wants to see integrity in the way approval and disapproval is distributed to her and her siblings. For instance, if you value tidiness then be sure to tell her when you are happy with her efforts and be sure to match those yourself. Just because children may not hold their parents to account for moments of hypocrisy doesn't mean they don't see them!

She needs you to acknowledge that other people and other families live their lives quite differently from yours. As she changes and gradually decides how she wants to live her life - which might be different from yours, she wants you to support her explorations with a reasonable degree of tolerance and flexibility.

Sometimes parents can be over-exacting and will burst a bubble of excitement out of a desire to keep their daughter grounded. Of course, it is important to guard against her becoming arrogant but there are times when pure, unfettered celebration is absolutely called for. When your daughter comes home from school having won an award - this is a big moment for her. As a parent you can so easily damage her by being too rigorous in questioning her what the reward was for - how many other children got the same reward, how often does the teacher give them out? and so on. Before you know where you are, you have turned a huge positive into a moment of doubt and even humiliation.

Secondary school age

We have seen that what your daughter wants, in terms of validation, is for your engagement and acknowledgment to be heartfelt and meaningful. When we apply that advice to parenting girls at secondary school, things can get harder. Your daughter may not be particularly easy to praise and finding genuine opportunities for connection can become less common for a while.

At this age, parenting becomes more about emotional validation than guiding moral behaviour. She needs to know that you understand the complex and sometimes painful emotional landscape she is travelling through and that her feelings are normal and not weird. So, just listening to her problems with earnestness and empathy is the validation she needs now. As she tells you the story of her day she is telling you not because you need to know but because she needs to tell you. You should listen and comment with gentle endorsements which recognise the tricky emotional journey her day has been. Emotional validation can come through comments like, 'That sounds really tough for you,' or 'I wonder how that makes you feel?' and 'Yes, I can see how that made you feel those things.' Make her feel that she has your full attention at that moment, that her troubles are worthy of respect and acknowledgment.

It can be a good idea to hold these conversations while out walking or in the car so that there is limited eye contact or face-to-face dialogue. That often really helps young people come out of their shell and express themselves differently and more powerfully.

During the process of listening it can be really hard to resist the idea of giving advice. You need to tread carefully! If you offer platitudes, advice you have given many times before, or the first piece of advice that comes into your head, this will seriously undermine your credibility as advice-giver and can feel insulting to your daughter. However well-meaning, an ill-considered remark delivered at the wrong moment can make her feel like you are just not listening and therefore don't care. Latching on to the wrong part of the story can also create frustration and make her less likely to bring problems to you in the future.

One good rule of thumb might be to always offer rather than give advice: 'I have heard everything you have just said and it sounds like things are really tough for you right now. There are things I could say to you that might help; do you want me to share my thoughts?'

Don't be offended if she says no! We have seen that girls' understanding of friendship turbulence is generally more sophisticated than we credit them for. Offering her a supportive conversational space to explore the problem will more likely lead to her discovering her own solution, than you trying to come up with an answer that perfectly fits the convoluted situation she is in.

Showing that you believe she is capable of resolving emotional difficulties will make her feel grown up and more in control of her problems. She may be curious to know what your advice is, but crucially she needs to be able to turn this down without ending the conversation. Often she is not looking for advice, but simply wants the opportunity to elaborate on her own story.

When you feel there is a need to offer specific guidance, a useful approach can be to wrap it in a question. For example:

"I'm sure you've already thought about this problem from Sophie's perspective. Did that help you to understand what went wrong or what to do next?'

Here, you are inviting your daughter to share more about her problem (as opposed to giving advice), whilst also being respectful and not patronising. If she has not yet thought about the problem from Sophie's point of view, the question will prompt her to do so now.

Where you are giving advice, check yourself; are you just lecturing her? Is the advice something she already knows or something you have told her already many times before? There is nothing worse than being lectured. Lecturing is a one-sided conversation presented by an expert to a student, and taking this approach will reinforce the power dynamic in which you position yourself as the expert in girls' friendship issues. In reality, she is the expert! It is your role to be a reflective and non-judgmental listener.

At the end of the process – when she has nothing more to say – you should find a pleasant distraction. Talk about something that makes her feel good; recall a happy memory, or talk about something she is good at. Look forward to an upcoming sport fixture, concert or trip. Maybe sit on the sofa and watch a favourite movie together. Give her the chance to move on and heal. After a few hours or the next day, she may want to talk again, this time with a different perspective and she may seek your advice and rehearse strategies with you. This time, you can engage more in a dialogue and steer her towards the best outcome. Equally, she may have come up with her own solutions.

However, avoid chasing for news. A daughter who has done a lot of sharing and then agreed a strategy for the next day, has the right to move on without any further feedback or mention. She will give you an update when she is ready. Putting pressure on her to disclose how the day went is not helpful. This is an opportunity to show that you respect that her problems and issues belong to her and not to you. It can be very tempting to want to follow up and build on the closeness experienced the day before, to hear more about the other girls and whether or not the agreed strategy was successful. But her friendship problems are inherently complex and the day that has just passed is unknowable for you. Many things will have happened that might have totally eclipsed the events of the previous day. The desire to repeat the extended sharing of the evening before needs to come from her, not you. A simple and normal enquiry of, 'How was your day?', is the best way to normalise things again but at the same time leaving the door open to further conversation.

Finding the balance

Your daughter wants you to be close but also respectful of her space.

She wants you to acknowledge her experimental identities but also to be unafraid to guide her when they go too far.

She wants you to defend her and be her champion, but not to embarrass her or become over-involved.

She will want time alone but to remain connected.

She wants freedom but not to be abandoned.

She needs you to acknowledge her existential pain but not be panicked by it.

What not to do

The idea of offering rather than giving advice may feel counter-intuitive to some parents. It is therefore worth exploring why this is such an important idea.

Parents often find themselves giving advice such as:

'Have you tried talking to her/them?'

'I think you should forgive and forget and move on.'

'There are plenty of other girls in the school – make new friends.'

'When I was at school we didn't have any of this sort of thing going on.'

'I just think you should put your mobile phone away and do something else.'

'How do you want me to fix this? Shall I ring the school? Shall I ring the parents of the mean girls?'

'I just think these other girls are horrible and I don't even know why you want to hang out with them.'

'Perhaps you should have thought twice before being friends with Sofia again.'

'I know Jessica's mum and I can't believe Jessica would say things like that to you.'

'All this socialising and the problems that go with it are getting in the way of you getting good grades, young lady. I suggest you focus on more important things.'

'Why don't we have some of your friends for a sleepover and you can have a good time – but only two.'

'Just because everyone else has the same shoes as each other doesn't make your shoes "horrible and disgusting".'

'My friend has a daughter in the year below you, why don't you see if you can make friends with her.'

'I'll talk to your teacher again and see what we can do to sort all this out.'

'Your sister never had these problems.'

'Have you thought about this from the other girls' point of view?'

'Do you think this is about your hormones?'

'This is just a phase you are going through; it'll pass.'

'It's probably just because this other girl is jealous of you.'

'Why don't you just try to not let it worry you?'

'Why don't you show me all the text messages you have and we'll go through each one, including what you replied with.'

Try reading these pieces of advice again but this time imagine you are a young girl, anxious about her friendships. Does even a single one of these comments actually make you feel reassured, more confident or empowered? Rather, the girl is likely to feel belittled, confused, angry, patronised and misunderstood. She may disguise her deep sense of hopelessness, despair and betrayal at her parent's ineptitude and continue to smile and behave well, but inside she is boiling.

As adults, we sometimes have to ask ourselves, what is the motive behind the advice we are giving? While painful to acknowledge, sometimes our comments have the intention of reassuring ourselves (papering over the problem, offering a quick fix) rather than being of any real benefit to the girl.

Girls can easily feel patronised by the poor quality of advice being proffered. They are not in a position to challenge your advice without appearing insolent and rude. Imagine if she came back to you with,

"Sorry, Mum/Dad, but that has got to be one of the most simplistic, idiotic, useless and frankly insulting pieces of advice ever offered to anyone by anyone – I really think you should try harder. Go on, have another go, but remember I am judging you for all eternity by what comes out of your mouth next."

OK, that's a little extreme, but the stakes are high and what you say (and don't say) in these situations matters. The short-to-medium term future of your relationship with your daughter depends on what happens in these moments.

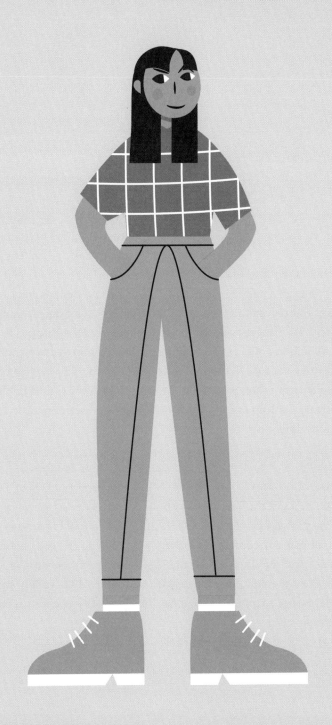

Over-reacting and under-reacting

Some parents tend to overreact to anything their daughter tells them that can be judged as a problem. They don't cope well with the idea that their daughter is not always happy and perfectly behaved, or at least they may see these moments as 'issues to be fixed'. They will phone the school to complain, or phone the parents of other children to fight their daughter's cause. They will be blinkered in their interpretation of their daughter's issue and make summary and immutable judgements about other girls and their actions. The word 'bullying' is often over and incorrectly used and what started as their daughter feeling a little upset and anxious can quickly escalate into a full-scale incident. Daughters of over-reacting parents quickly learn to downplay the story of their day because over-reaction is so unhelpful. This can lead them to decide not to tell their parent of a situation which is genuine but low risk. **Parental over-reaction is a significant barrier to communication from the girl's point of view.**

Some parents under-react and struggle to engage with their daughter's friendship issues. This may be because of a lack of attention or a lack of time or it may be because the parent does not understand the significance of the issues. The parent fails to recognise the girl's existential imperative to have and maintain close friends. It can be very hard for a girl whose parent is unwilling to listen carefully and with compassion to the problems she needs to share. The daughter of an under-reacting parent will naturally tend to exaggerate her issues to prompt a response; this leads to inaccurate and ineffective communication.

Contacting the school

It is useful here to talk about your relationship with your daughter's school when it comes to friendship turbulence. If your daughter is very upset it is only natural for you to experience an emotional response yourself. But objectivity and a cool head are needed at this point if you are to prevent yourself, unwittingly, from making the situation worse. If you think she is being bullied then you can find some specific advice in Appendix 1. However, what follows is useful to read before you assume that bullying is taking place.

A parent needs to remember that successful education is a partnership between home and school. It is vital that communication is conducted in a courteous and constructive manner. Aggressive and demanding emails and phone calls simply make things worse for the girls and make the teachers' job even harder. Parents who demand punishment and retribution create a dynamic of tension and hostility which suddenly becomes the focus of everyone's energy and attention; disputes between the girls ironically then take a back seat. When seen from the girls' point of view, conflict between the parent and the teachers often means that the views of the daughter are ignored; sometimes with very detrimental consequences.

Scenario

Phone call from parent to school: "I am deeply concerned that you have not punished the girls who have been excluding my daughter; I now want to speak to your line manager."
Teacher: "Following your complaint, I looked at this situation in great detail. We did a lot of talking and the girls, including your daughter, all seemed happy when they went home."
Parent: 'Well, she is in her bedroom right now, crying her eyes out. Whatever the school has done has made things worse"

Meanwhile, the girl crying in her bedroom is thinking, "Why did I let the grown-ups get involved? This is so much worse now; everyone is shouting and I just wanted Alesha to be a bit nicer to me and not spend all her time with Phoebe. Alesha and Phoebe have fallen out now anyway, so it is all just a complete mess. I can't tell my parent the truth because I would just look so silly and they would be angry with me."

Another example:
Parent, "Those girls are so cruel. I'm calling their mothers."
Daughter, "Wait? What? No, don't do that!"
Parent, "It's too late, this has gone too far."
Daughter, "I'm going to my room."

Daughter thinks but does not say, "My life is over. There is no way any of those girls will ever speak to me again if I get them into trouble with their parents. I think I'll go on the internet now and see how easy it is to change school."

Calling the other parent(s) to complain can be extremely damaging. Whether the other parent decides to support or criticise their daughter, the potential for reconciliation between the two girls is severely reduced. Parents find themselves saying condemnatory things which are hard to come back from and which just add to ongoing conflict between girls and groups of girls. Parents will often also get angry with each other and then insist that their daughters have 'nothing to do with that girl.' As if in school you can actually completely avoid other students! Anyway, who's to say the girls might not have become the best of friends just hours later – if only the parent hadn't tried to fix their problem?

If you are the parent who receives the angry phone call, try your utmost to remain neutral and calm. Try not to get drawn into an argument despite provocation. Tell the other parent you will talk to your daughter, thank them for getting in touch and end the call. It is probably wise not to return the call even if you discover that your daughter's behaviour has not been exemplary.

Modelling

While this is not always easy, modelling good relational attitudes to fellow human beings is an important part of parenting your daughter. Children copy what they see rather than what they're told. It is helpful to be honest with yourself about the way you talk about other people. Is the language you use and the attitude you project what you would want your daughter to replicate? For instance, if you are in the habit of moaning about your boss at work, or being very critical of colleagues, or tending to dwell on negatives, think about the message that is giving your daughter.

Finally

Finally, a word of encouragement if you are reading this whilst in the middle of troubled times in your daughter's friendships. She'll get through this – just sit with her and hang on! Holding on to the hope and knowledge that things will improve when she can't see that for herself is very powerful. This can be achieved by simply sticking with her, being by her side through the hard times. Support her, love her, listen to her and empower her; she will find her own way.

CHAPTER EIGHT

Mediation, and how teachers can make things worse

Coming up in this chapter:

"...the way that most teachers go about trying to resolve conflict between girls does not work well; it takes up a lot of time and does not lead to lasting harmony."

When girls fall out it can reach a level of upset where teachers are required to get involved. This might be because girls ask for support, the classroom teaching is disrupted by the turmoil or because a parent rings to express concern. Sometimes when the conflict is particularly oppositional and both sides are very angry, the teacher is positioned as impartial adjudicator, expected to hand down a judgment of where blame lies and deliver sanctions.

This is a Justice Tools approach. Teachers spend time investigating, taking written statements, trying to apportion blame, making judgements and writing reports. This approach rarely if ever makes things better for the girls because it is based on a false assumption: because one girl is upset, somebody else must have done something wrong.

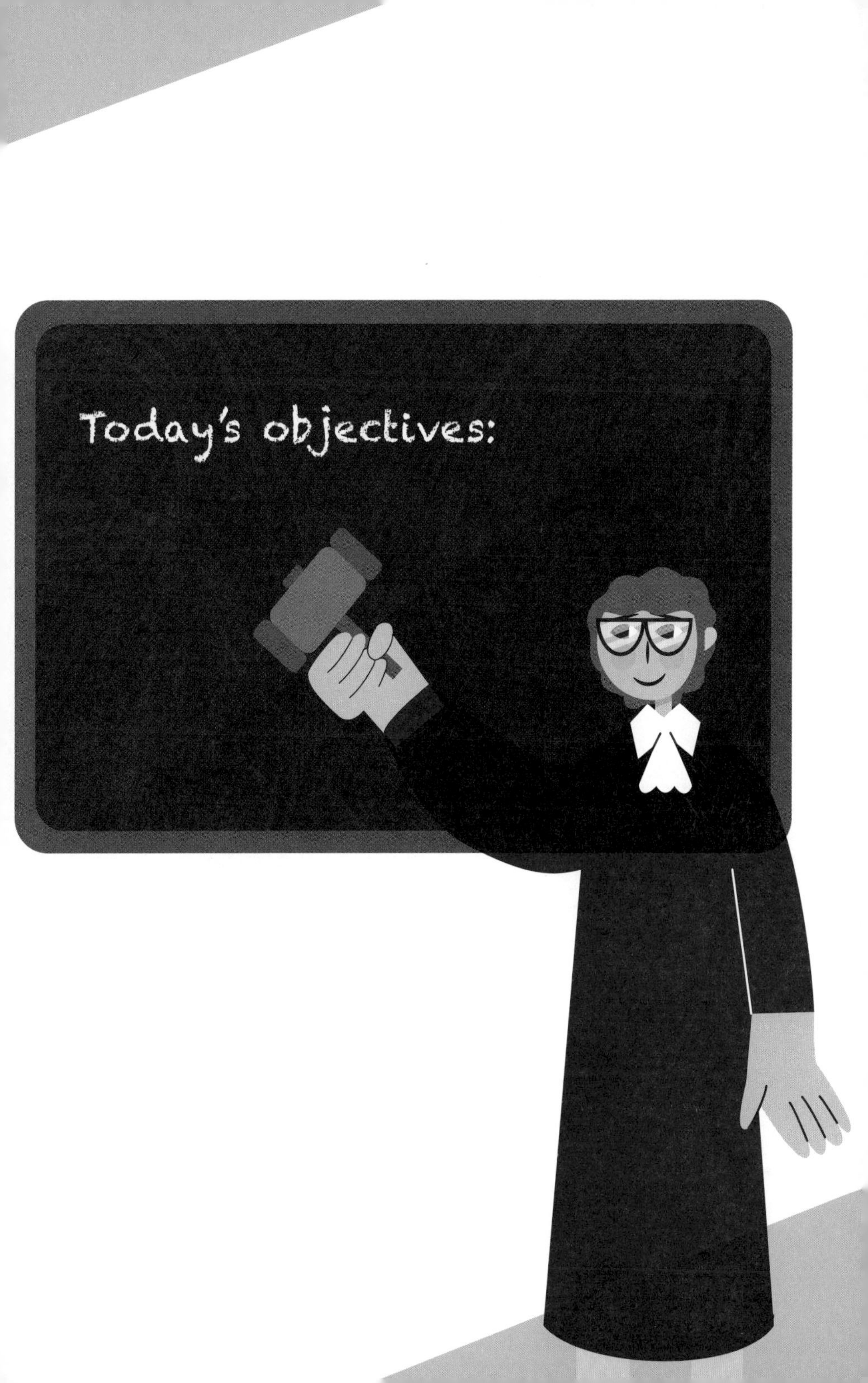
Today's objectives:

Parents have varying degrees of understanding about how teachers can support girls in their friendships. Many parents assume that teachers have a lot of influence and can – or should - be 'sorting things out' between the girls. However, their expectations of what teachers can achieve are often unrealistic. This chapter will examine the impossibility of the teacher's role as a judge and consider the situation from their point of view. Broadly, the tasks they face fall into three categories:

1. working out what really went wrong
2. taking actions that actually improve the situation for the girls involved
3. meeting parental expectations

Working out what really went wrong

In previous chapters we have examined the difficulties of communication and understanding between parents and girls; these also apply to teachers in school. To recap:

Fluidity

Friendships between girls are often very fluid. Two girls may be falling out one minute and be the best of friends the next. Indeed, this can turn into a pattern of behaviour between them over time making their relationship very hard to support or even understand. Girls need room to get things off their chest, to vent their disappointment or even anger without that meaning they won't be friends again. Some friendships are so fluid that it is impossible for adults to keep up.

Complexity

The issues within friendships are often very complex and hard to express. There may be multiple 'players' within each scenario, each with their own agenda and motivation. Adults listening to a girl describing a falling-out may find the narrative hard to follow.

Not the whole truth

Girls may not always tell a complete version of the truth and may omit parts of the story where they themselves might be accused of wrongdoing. Girls will tend to portray their story in a way that is designed to manipulate the adults' understanding, for the numerous reasons outlined in Chapter 5.

Generational disconnect
Adults can find it very difficult to understand the context of conflict and hurt for young people. This can include issues surrounding social media platforms, fashion trends, the use of language and whatever is 'cool' at the time.

As a result of these barriers, it is practically impossible for the teacher to gain a truly accurate understanding of what went wrong between the girls. They hear only what the girls choose to tell them, and any judgement they hand down is necessarily based on a limited, and often flawed, understanding of events. Given this constraint, handing out sanctions is risky and can leave teachers open to criticism if a different version of events is later revealed.

Taking actions that actually improve the situation for the girls involved
In reality then, it is not surprising that teachers rarely do deliver definitive judgements. Instead they seek to mediate, using established methods such as 'Conflict Resolution' and 'Restorative Practice'. These mediation sessions tend to result in universal statements about forgiveness and being kind. Where they have to apportion blame they will often compromise and find mild fault on both sides. They have to be aware of the need for impartiality, maintain trust with their pupils and bear in mind other pressures on their time, all the while being seen to 'do something' to fix disputes. These conflicting pressures can mean they reach conclusions that can end up sounding woolly and patronising, such as:

- "I think we have learned that you can both be a bit over-sensitive."
- "In life, words matter and you need to think carefully about the effect your words can have on others."
- "We all have to get on with each other in this school; we are a community that cares for every individual."
- "In future, perhaps you should both take a moment to consider the feelings of the other before assuming the worst."
- "I'm glad that you have both shown the strength and maturity to understand each other's point of view and indeed, apologise for your parts in this upset."

All of the above summary statements may seem reasonable and neutral but in reality the girls hearing those words will feel patronised, disconnected, frustrated, disillusioned, judged and annoyed. They will never tell the teacher that is how they feel, but they will go to great lengths to avoid having to sit through such a session again. The teacher may well interpret that lack of need to repeat mediation sessions as a sign of success - it isn't!

Meeting parents' expectations

Parents often have expectations that justice will be delivered for perceived relational aggression and upset. In trying to meet these expectations, teachers face a number of problems.

As we have seen, teachers will tend to reach compromises with general comments that apply to all involved. Many parents will not be satisfied by these concluding reports which they may see as platitudinous and lacking clarity. It is not uncommon, even when mediation has been successful in bringing girls together, for the parent to undo the benefits and demand more from the school. In demanding more, a parent needs to consider whether the expectation that their daughter should never experience any unhappiness is dominating their parenting decisions. No one goes through life, especially adolescence, without experiencing unhappiness. The role of the parent is to support and comfort, not to mend, blame and overprotect.

It is by no means all parents who will take the view described above. Some may be happy to receive the rather cautious and fence-sitting email or phone call. But the proof of whether the mediation was successful will only be known when the daughter comes home. If the daughter takes a very different view of the outcome of the mediation session from the teacher, then the teacher loses credibility and neither the parent nor daughter are likely to trust offers of support again in the future.

De-skilling through the creation of co-dependency

As a mediation session concludes, a teacher will often decide to re-state that their services remain accessible and useful: "Next time things flare up, why don't you let me know and we'll sit down for a catch up." Many girls will interpret this remark as the teacher wishing to make themselves indispensable. The girls will sense that if their friendship issues are successfully resolved, the teacher will take credit - at least in the staffroom and with the leadership of the school. The remark de-skills the girls. It says, 'In future, if you have friendship unhappiness always come to me and I will fix it.' That may not be the intention behind the remark but there is always the danger of an unhealthy co-dependency here:

The teacher feels valued and valuable by making the girls happy; the girls want approval and validation from the teacher and so bring them their problems.

The notion that girls should always seek adult help rather than solving issues for themselves is one that needs very careful thought.

Conclusion

Schools strive to find lasting and effective ways to support girls in their friendships but mediation does not appear to be the best answer. In Chapter 9 we will look at what happens when a school prompts and promotes the power of empathy and how that can have a profound effect on the way friendships are conducted.

CHAPTER NINE

The Power of Empathy

Coming up in this chapter:

"Empathy has the capacity to help girls work through challenging emotions such as jealousy and fear of isolation."

Kindness and its limitations

The idea of preaching kindness in schools is very popular. As a way of ensuring good behaviour, embedding a culture of kindness in a school is designed to create harmony and prevent conflict both on an individual and community level. The word 'kindness' is often one of the key words in a school's mission statement along with 'respect', 'excellence' and 'achievement'. Pupils, especially in Primary Schools, attend assemblies and lessons in which kindness is explained and insisted upon as the overriding moral ideal.

However, kindness has varying effectiveness as a tool for preventing, analysing and resolving conflict in school. This chapter will take a look at the limitations of kindness and offer a more evolved and sophisticated tool – empathy.

Engaging in an act of kindness can be a pleasant and warm experience itself, and if one person is kind to another then they can expect that kindness to be returned. Both giving and receiving kindness is beneficial to the individual. Kindness then spreads to become the normal way in which everyone at the school relates to everyone else. Kindness is a currency which, when exchanged, creates a community that is happy and stable; a reciprocal contract of kindness-sharing exists between all members. Achieving this state is beneficial for everyone and so it is easy to see why schools promote the idea that everyone must agree to strive to be kind. Kindness is a worthy ideal.

However, the community of kindness is fragile. Forces such as jealousy, rivalry, frustration, insecurity, damaged dignity, intolerance, anger, bitterness, selfishness, ego and unfairness arise on a daily basis in schools (and life) and are unavoidable and incredibly powerful. These forces occur naturally and are normal and inevitable elements of social interaction and friendship. Crucially, these forces occur even when everyone has been kind and this therefore questions the idea that kindness is a comprehensive moral code. Kindness doesn't have much to offer to an individual experiencing bitterness, jealousy or insecurity and so its power is limited.

Let's take an example: a teacher simply asks children in the class to form pairs for a collaborative task that will last the afternoon. Inevitably, in a friendship group of three girls, two girls form a pair and the third is left to work with someone else. The two girls who formed the pair reluctantly separate from the third, but enjoy an afternoon of laughter and fun. The third girl has to work with a boy she doesn't get on with and she has a miserable afternoon. In an act of kindness, the two other girls commiserate with the third girl at the end of the day and attempt to cheer her up, but it is not enough and just makes her feel worse. Negative forces such as unfairness, bitterness, jealousy, insecurity and frustration start to act on the third girl and she goes home feeling really unhappy. The two other girls were not unkind in being the lucky ones who got to be part of the pair, and they did nothing wrong by enjoying their afternoon. Similarly, the teacher has not been unkind either, and may well feel that it was good for the girls to experience some independence rather than being constantly 'joined at the hip'. Kindness has not worked in this situation. The event, and the forces that came with it, have left a scar on the third girl that may worsen over time and lead to friendship conflict. In this example we see how, even in a community where everyone strives to be kind, conflict and unhappiness can arise easily and kindness is often not powerful enough to overcome negative forces.

Therefore, kindness has its limits as a tool for social harmony and it often fails to both prevent and resolve conflict. When schools over-emphasise kindness it can seem reductive, patronising and meaningless for pupils; asking them to be kind is pointing to a simple moral code of behaviour that was well established in their minds from the age of 4 or 5. The constant repetition of the call for kindness weakens the message until it becomes like white noise. It does not leave them empowered to deal with the negative forces that act upon the kindness community.

What is empathy and why does it help?

Empathy: the ability to understand and share the feelings of another.

When you evoke empathy in girls, you prompt them to feel what others are feeling and experiencing. This has the power to change their thinking and behaviour profoundly. Empathy helps girls to think about their friendships more objectively, rather than only from their own point of view; they identify the feelings they have in common with others and ask themselves: 'If I was feeling like that, what would I want to happen?'. Returning to our example above, if the two girls engaged empathy rather than kindness, they may stop and ask themselves what it must have been like to have been the one left out. They might then strategise to prevent such hurt in future. They may make a pact within their group of three to rotate the one being left out, or they may lobby the teacher to allow them to work in a three. Above all, when situations like that arise again, they will all make explicit their awareness of how painful and upsetting it can be. Having empathy for a peer who is upset helps the girls show each other more targeted, focused and effective support.

While empathy helps girls to understand why a friend is upset, it can also help the upset friend to understand her situation. For example, if our third girl in the story above is encouraged to empathise, putting herself in the shoes of her friends, she may recognise that what appeared to be an afternoon of fun and laughter was perhaps not as rosy as it seemed from the outside. They were just doing school-work after all. She may be better able to remember times when the other girls had felt left out and how it felt when she had been one of the pair.

Susan Lanzoni, in her book 'The History of Empathy' (Yale University 2018), traces the history of the word empathy and its sociological, political and psychological significance. The definition of the word is contested but she offers: 'empathy [...] comprises a complex, artful but also effortful practice that involves feelings, intellect and imagination'. Lanzoni and others have argued that empathy is not merely a feeling waiting to emerge as soon as heightened emotions die down, but a thinking process involving application, focus and work. It is a skill we all need to continually work on throughout life.

Empathy is something that can and should be discussed, evoked and promoted. In order to get a group of girls to feel empathy for one another it can be very helpful to provide a stimulus to remind them or educate them in this aspect of social engagement. Empathy, being far more nuanced and complex than concepts such as kindness, has greater capacity to help girls work through challenging emotions such as jealousy and fear of isolation.

In the next Chapter we look at an approach adopted by schools that naturally evokes empathy and empowers girls to resolve their friendship turbulence for themselves.

CHAPTER TEN

Girls on Board

Coming up in this chapter:

"...embedding the Girls on Board approach becomes a way of ensuring self-generating empathy and the self-regulation of relationally aggressive behaviours."

So far we have looked at the difficulties girls, parents and teachers face when girls fall out at school. We have looked at the features and causes of normal-if-painful friendship turbulence. We have also examined the common techniques used by teachers and parents to support girls through friendship upsets that are usually of limited effectiveness. So, the next question has to be: how can schools do better to support girls when they fall out, and how does that help you as a parent?

For some years now, many schools have adopted a different approach to supporting girls in their friendships: *Girls on Board*. This approach is applied from Year 3 upwards. When a school adopts the *Girls on Board* approach it undertakes to stop using the justice tools approach and mediation (outlined in Chapter 8), and to replace them with *Girls on Board* sessions.

Girls on Board schools will have several teachers who have undertaken training to become Champions of the approach. The training takes five hours of study and can be undertaken at face-to-face events or online.

What follows is an outline of what the *Girls on Board* approach is and how it works.

The Girls on Board approach in a nutshell

Girls on Board is an approach adopted by schools and understood by parents which empowers girls to resolve their friendship issues for themselves. It does this by evoking the power of empathy through teacher-led, non-judgemental sessions which are called in response to things going wrong for the girls.

Girls on Board does NOT:

- provide a way to prevent girls ever falling out with each other – that would be impossible! It does, however, give them the vocabulary and framework to work things out for themselves, and that reduces the frequency and severity of fallouts.
- suggest that, because the role of adults in this approach is relatively recessive, girls should not talk to or share their problems with adults. Quite the reverse, the approach encourages girls to continue to seek help and support from adults. It guides adults to support rather than interfere, and to respond in ways that focus on empowering the girls, rather than trying to 'fix' their problems.

A school will launch the *Girls on Board* approach with a single 50 minute session with the girls (or several shorter sessions for the younger girls). At the same time a Parent Guide is sent to parents so they understand what is happening. Having read the first 9 chapters of this book, you are already very familiar with this approach because, essentially, *When Girls Fall Out* is based on the thinking that gave rise to *Girls on Board*. The content of the sessions is designed to hold up a mirror to the way friendships are formed and operated. It is a reflective and non-didactic approach where the teacher/facilitator will often offer each new idea with, "Isn't it true to say that…" So, for instance:

- "Isn't it true to say that every girl between the ages of 7 and 18 must have someone to call her friend, in her year group and in her school?"

- "Isn't it true that when your three friends are inviting you to join them for a sleepover, but you can't come, it is generally hard for them to decide whether or not to go ahead?"
- "Isn't it true that girls often talk to the family pet to find that all important 'person' to talk to who isn't going to judge or offer unwanted advice?"

Through role-play and other discussion topics the girls quickly realise two things:

1. The teacher/facilitator is not there to teach them how to be a good friend, or endlessly revisit the topic of kindness-to-all. The teacher/facilitator really does 'get' girl friendships and is here to share what it is actually like being a girl at school.
2. The girls (pretty much) ALL share feelings of anxiety about finding trusting and reliable friendships to a greater or lesser extent.

This leads the girls to realise that the best way to help themselves and each other feel more secure in their friendships is for them to work it out between themselves. The adults will support, but not interfere.

The facilitator invites the girls to reflect that:

- things tend to get worse when adults get involved in friendship issues,
- some girls have parents who over-react and some who under-react,
- a girl-in-the-water will only find a new friendship group as a result of other girls including her,
- there are various types of behaviour, such as 'Queen Bee', that can lead to upset and unhappiness,
- girls tend to form friendships in group sizes of 2, 3, 4 and 5,
- when a girl's friends all go the loo without her it can make her anxious,
- girls often don't tell the whole truth to their parents.

In fact, even before the approach is introduced at a school, the girls already know pretty much everything that has been written about in this book - just ask them!

In a *Girls on Board* session, the teacher is not offering new information or insights. Instead the teacher demonstrates to the girls how much they already know about friendships.

As a result of attending a *Girls on Board* session, something very profound changes in the thinking of the girls. They become more empathetic with each other's plight. Perhaps even more than that, they realise that in order to find what they each want - trusting and reliable friendships - they need to acknowledge to themselves and each other that that is their common goal. The realisation of how normal and common these feelings are evokes empathy in the group. They show empathy through their actions of reconciliation, forgiveness and renewal. Empathy becomes a part of who they are, how they behave towards each other, what it means to be a girl in their peer group. In this way, embedding the *Girls on Board* approach becomes a way of ensuring self-generating empathy and the self-regulation of relationally aggressive behaviours.

Girl empowerment is achieved through the revelation that it is only the girls themselves that can find effective resolutions to their conflicts; all that remains is for the adults to get out of the way so that those resolutions can be found and acted upon.

Girls on Board at home

Girls on Board is an approach available to all schools to sign up to. More information can be found at GirlsonBoard.co.uk. However, if your school does not currently offer this approach, here's how you can be more *"Girls on Board"* at home.

Use what you have learnt from this book to demonstrate to your daughter that you understand friendship issues from her point of view. This will gain you credibility and she will trust you more. For instance, talk to her about what you learnt in Chapter 2 about group sizes and listen to her opinion. Share your understanding of Chapter 3 and the different forms of girl behaviour and see if she has other ones to add to the list.

Here's a scenario you can share with her: let's say she is walking down a corridor in a group of three friends, side by side. Up ahead she sees that the corridor narrows and each side is lined with male staff. She and her friends are going to need to go in single file. Ask her where she would prefer to go? Front, middle or back?

If she says she would opt to go at the front, explore the reasons why. You may find her saying it is because,

- it doesn't matter where anyone goes, so she might as well lead the way,
- her friends are not very decisive and it would be better if she took charge of this potentially embarrassing situation,
- she is happy to lead the way this time but she might ask someone else to take that extra responsibility next time.

If she says she would rather go in the middle, again explore the reasons. She may say it is because,

- it feels safer in the middle,
- she remains more connected to her two friends,
- she would just rather someone else took responsibility,
- the girl in front and the girl behind can't have a conversation without her knowing what is being said.

If she says she would rather go at the back, you might find her saying it is because,

- it is polite to let others go first,
- she and her friends find decision making very hard and she is happy to tag along rather than risk further disagreements about potential decisions that need to be made,
- she feels more secure being able to keep her two friends in her eye-line,
- this is where she always goes when they have to line up.

Whatever her reaction, you are not there to judge or comment other than to show an interest; see where the conversation leads. If she is reluctant to engage in this conversation, perhaps offer what you might have done when you were her age (mother), or how men feel about something like this (father). That might prompt the conversation to go further.

Going to the loo is another daily occurrence to talk about too. Do she and her friends go to the loo together? If not, how does it feel when she comes out of the loo and her friends have disappeared? Do her friends have an agreement about moments like this - perhaps when one girl is in a different class for the morning, or half the group go off to play a sports fixture?

All these things are typical topics for Girls-on-Board-type discussions. They all demonstrate an understanding that girls can experience a degree of anxiety about friendships from moment to moment, and that can add up to a lot of stress over time. When things actually go wrong, when there is tension, misunderstanding, jealousy or just general friendship turbulence, these moments become absolutely crucial.

The fact that you have had these conversations with her already will prove to her that you understand. You will have shown that you are willing to take seriously the minute nature of events that can cause uncertainty and upset; you have normalised rather than trivialised. You are already on the same page, ready and willing to listen and share.

Girls on Board makes girls realise that when they fall out with each other it is completely normal and not weird and scary.

CHAPTER ELEVEN

Looking at the principles that underpin Girls on Board

Coming up in this chapter:

" Nearly all the problems that girls have in their friendships stem from this one, central truth: Every girl fears isolation profoundly."

In Chapter 10 we looked at how the *Girls on Board* approach empowers girls in school to resolve their friendship issues for themselves. This chapter illustrates and recaps the principles we have talked about in this book so far, and how they can be applied through the *Girls on Board* approach in schools. By sharing a narrative of girl friendship turbulence at school, we hope to consolidate your understanding of some key points made in this book and how *Girls on Board* can help.

Every girl needs a friend.

In this story we see an illustration of how important it is for every girl that they have at least one girl in their peer group they can call their friend. First of all, we look at the example of fears around joining a new school, especially mid-year, and then the scenario of what happens when friends move away.

Emma has always found it hard to make friends at school. Her interests are unusual and it can feel hard to find commonalities with other girls. Because her parents moved house halfway through a school year, she had to join a new school where all the girl friendship groups had already been formed. On her first day, however, she meets and makes friends with Jameelah and they become the best of pals. Jameelah is also a girl who has not always found it easy to form friendships, being rather shy and quiet. The girls get on so well they come to rely on each other for company and friendship throughout the school day and into the evenings and weekends on social media.

Then comes the news that Jameelah's family is moving away and she will no longer be attending the same school as Emma. Emma is devastated and no amount of advice, cajoling, encouragement, love and attention from home can stop her feeling that her world has collapsed. The thought of being alone at school, without a friend to sit next to, have lunch with, walk the corridors next to - is more than she can bear.

As we have seen earlier in the book, it is hard for some adults to acknowledge just how significant this first principle is. To understand girls of this age it is the foremost principle to grasp, acknowledge and assume. Nearly all the problems that girls have in their friendships stem from this one, central truth: Every girl fears isolation profoundly.

It is with the restatement of this truth that every *Girls on Board* session begins. The *Girls on Board* facilitator takes a few moments to let this truth sink in; the girls ponder its significance and begin to re-bond around its comforting and reassuring commonality.

Girls need to find things to bond over.

It is sometimes the case that girls find integration hard and they need to understand how friendships are formed.

Once Jameelah has left the school, Emma struggles to find new friendships. She seeks help from pastoral care staff at her school. They point out that friendships between people, whatever gender or age group, very often form around areas of common interest. Because two people enjoy watching movies, they become friends. The things people bond over and form friendship around may be significant – like both are champion swimmers, or it may be more 'everyday' – they both love particular computer games. Emma learns this important life lesson and begins to build interests that other girls also have. Emma learns that she needs to maintain an open mind and prioritise relating to others in order to start building these connections.

It is important to remember that staff operating within the *Girls on Board* approach will find there are still plenty of moments when good advice and guidance is useful and needed. Helping girls to understand how friendships are formed definitely falls into that category.

Don't ever assume you know the full story, and mediation between girls rarely works

In this next part of the story, conflict arises and we show how hard it is to get to the full truth and how mediation, without the full truth, can sometimes be damaging.

Thankfully, Emma has found some friends. However, after a while, she and her group of friends hear that other girls are talking about them, making remarks that are designed to be mean and hurtful.

Unsure what to do, Emma and her friends turn to pastoral care staff at school and their parents at home. Because Emma's school does not follow the *Girls on Board* approach, staff begin a forensic investigation of who said what to whom, when and why. They call various groups of girls together and hear increasingly confused and varying stories. In the end, the consensus seems to point to one particular girl – Tara - and Tara is reprimanded for being mean.

Meanwhile the parents of all the girls that were gathered together by staff have been hearing their daughter's versions of events. Each parent takes their own view of where the truth lies. Some remain detached from the whole situation, preferring instead first to offer their daughter some kindness and support, and then distract her. Other parents over-react; some decide to phone the parents of girls they consider to be at fault, others ring the school and demand action to 'stamp out bullying'. Emma is reasonably content that her cause has been heard, but she remains worried that Tara has received a reprimand when her behaviour has been no worse than others.

Tara is very upset at being reprimanded and her parents meet with the Head of Year to complain. The Head of Year does more investigation but is unable to unearth any further credible evidence from the girls other than more stories that create yet more fog and confusion. Reluctantly the Head of Year tells the parents that the reprimand stands, though offers plenty of ongoing support for Tara. Although Tara appears happy at school, she remains very upset at home, and her parents complain again. They say that the school's unjustified actions have damaged Tara's confidence and self-esteem and they threaten to withdraw her from the school. The school agonises over possible solutions to this given that Tara is demonstrably happy at school and when interviewed cannot provide an answer as to why she is unhappy at home. The real reason for Tara's unhappiness at home is that she overheard her parents saying that they thought she probably had been mean, despite them saying the opposite to the school. She feels unfairly judged and betrayed by her parents. In her view, the fight they are having with the school only makes things worse. In an attempt to make her parents feel sorry for her, Tara starts to accuse other girls of excluding her.

Frustrated with the school, Tara's parents take matters into their own hands and ring the parents of girls Tara says have been leaving her out. The parents of these girls tell them off and that causes the girls to produce counter-accusations which seem to show that Tara is lying to her parents. More and more parents complain to the school based on believing their daughter is telling them the whole truth. The school becomes increasingly involved in investigations which lead to further judgements and reprimands. Tara finds herself isolated by the other girls and refuses to go to school.

Tara's parents withdraw her from the school.

As the girls in her year group interpret all the events that led to Tara's departure, some consider the new order to be a victory. Others worry about how a girl who was essentially no different from any other and who behaved in the same way as every other girl has ended up rejected to the point of having to leave the school. Could they be next?

In this story the school and parents have adopted an approach which assumes that wrongdoing has occurred without sufficient certainty of the facts to justify making judgments; the judgements lead to reprimands and the reprimands lead to complaints. We see that, because the truth is too complex to grasp fully, mediation and investigation simply have made the situation worse. Mediation and investigation are not neutral acts, no matter how hard a staff member will try to allay fears of 'being in trouble'. What occurs between girls, their conversations, social media messages and general interactions are very subtle and nuanced; how each girl chooses to interpret the meaning of each interaction is subject to many factors, including how secure they are feeling about their friendships. (Indeed, all human interactions and relationships are a bit like that!)

Let's consider what might have happened if the school in our story was a *Girls on Board* school:

Because Emma's school embraces the *Girls on Board* approach, the staff listen carefully to Emma and her friends' story. The staff consider whether the story is consistent with bullying: is there clear evidence that one or more girls have victimised one girl consistently over time to make that girl unhappy? The staff quickly assess that this is not an instance of bullying and is normal-if-painful friendship turbulence. They realise that they are very unlikely ever to fully get to the truth of who said what to whom, when and why. Although Emma and her friends would quite like staff to speak to the other girls, staff advise them that that is not the approach they are going to take. Instead, using the *Girls on Board* triage approach, staff have the following three options:

1. Continue to listen and support, making themselves available in the future to listen again and reassess if needed, and offer advice if requested.

2. Call a *Girls on Board* session, getting the girls together from the whole year group and reminding them of the *Girls on Board* principles.
3. Offer individual girls counselling to help build coping and self-esteem strategies.

Staff decide to call a *Girls on Board* session and this empowers all the girls to talk through their issues after the session. Some conversations are face-to-face, some are via social media platforms. All the girls involved are aware that they must resolve the situation, not just for Emma but for all of them. Emma and her friends talk things through with Tara and her friends and issues are resolved. Staff are not involved in any of these negotiations and do not ask Emma or any of the girls how things are going. But they do observe how the girls are getting on from a distance and see that the friendship groups seem stable.

We come now to another important principle of *Girls on Board* - one that is particularly relevant for teachers whose job it is to manage girls' pastoral care: **If the story you are hearing does not point to bullying or specific wrongdoing, then do not attempt to use 'justice tools'.**

In this next episode of Emma's story we make the assumption, again, that Emma's school is now adopting the *Girls on Board* approach; we look at parental involvement and how important it is to use the *Girls on Board* triage system to assess whether or not to use **justice tools**.

Emma receives a social media message on Saturday evening saying, 'LOL Emma, yer mum's got fleas.' She is perturbed more than offended by this message, partly because it comes from a girl with whom she has an emerging friendship. She gets in touch with the sender of the message and receives a number of rather garbled messages in return, sent by various girls who are all obviously together. Again, she is not particularly upset by any of this but nonetheless shares the messages with her mother. Her mother brings a transcript of all the messages into school on Monday morning demanding that the staff investigate the disrespect shown to her personally and that the girl in question should be made to apologise to her and her daughter (Emma is mortified by her mother's reaction and vows never to share her social media dialogues again).

Being a *Girls on Board* school, Emma's Head of Year talks alone with Emma. Emma confirms that she was not offended and that she is struggling with her mother's over-reaction. The Head of Year rings Emma's mother and reminds her of the *Girls on Board* principles – that no bullying has taken place, the messages were a 'dare' and not designed to offend. Emma was not upset or offended and would much prefer that no further investigation or judgements were made. Trying to apportion blame and deliver justice would just make Emma's life awkward and possibly damage emerging and precious friendships.

Emma's mother is unhappy with the response of the Head of Year and complains to the Senior Leaders. Taking the *Girls on Board* approach, the Senior Leaders defend the Head of Year's judgement and continue to emphasise that as long as Emma is happy with the outcome there should be no perceived problem. Though she feels she has lost her argument with the school, the mother realises that Emma is happy and that further complaints might change that fact.

Schools not using the *Girls on Board* approach usually tackle girl friendship problems with their justice tools – the same tools they would habitually use to tackle wrongdoing. They use investigation, report summaries, judgments, sanctions, reprimands, restorative practice, mediation and monitoring. These strategies are simply ineffective when applied to normal-if-painful friendship turbulence and make the turbulence progressively worse over time, turning passing fluidity into chronic and systemic conflict. For some teachers, taking the recessive stance recommended by *Girls on Board* is counter-intuitive and so we need to understand more fully why justice tools don't work when tackling normal turbulence.

Justice tools are ineffective because the wrong moral code is being applied. We assume that because a girl has been upset by another girl that the aggressor has behaved badly and needs to be sanctioned. This seems on the surface to be logical and consistent with the whole concept of defining rules and sticking to them.

However, there are several problems with this way of thinking which we explored in Chapter 8. Adults applying 'justice tools' are merely being used as pawns in the game: complain to an adult and get the other girl told off. If you don't believe this, ask your daughter; she will confirm that most of the time, when adults get involved in girls' friendship issues, things get worse.

We must guard against the naïve assumption that the girl who appears to be upset is actually upset for the reasons she is claiming; she might even be using the adults as a tactic in normal-if-painful friendship turbulence. We should allow for the possibility that the level of upset expressed by a girl is proportionate to the amount of culpability she has in creating the circumstances that led to her apparent upset in the first place. In Emma's case, how certain are we that the apparently random message she received about her mother having fleas was not actually a reaction to something Emma said or messaged but which other girls have, for whatever reason, decided not to reveal?

Normal-if-painful friendship turbulence that falls short of the bullying threshold operates according to a different moral code: it is tit-for-tat low-level conflict – that's all. By using justice tools, we unwittingly underline moments of poor judgement on the part of girls. We go over past events, drawing undue attention to lapses in behaviour, rather than emphasising what is most important for the girls involved – building, maintaining and repairing friendships.

It may be fair to characterise the relational aggression within normal-if-regrettable friendship turbulence as 'mean', but that still does not imply that justice tools should be applied. Adult intervention will distort and contaminate the fine ebb and flow of girl relations which will nearly always right themselves if given the space, time and the *Girls on Board* approach.

Girls on Board does not stop girls falling out. We all fall out with each other from time to time, that's just an inevitable part of being alive. The *Girls on Board* approach is a way of limiting distress and healing hurt when they do fall out.

Once embedded in a school, the approach reduces the overall amount of falling out because girls are more willing and able to think through the consequences of conflict before things get too bad. Knowing that a *Girls on Board* session will be called if they can't sort out their conflict, the girls will do their best to prevent that happening, if only because calling a session is an admission that self-management is not working.

Girls on Board in action

This final part of Emma's story looks at a common scenario of girls falling out with each other and how, using the *Girls on Board* approach, staff manage to minimise the hurt and upset this might have caused.

Emma is now friends with Chloe and Kali, though the bond between them is not particularly strong. Emma accepts an invitation from Chloe to go shopping at the weekend, knowing that Kali has not been asked. Emma feels uncomfortable about this, but is caught in a dilemma - to reject the invitation and risk her friendship with Chloe, or accept the invitation and risk her friendship with Kali.

With some trepidation, Emma accepts Chloe's invitation and inevitably Kali finds out that she was excluded from the trip. On Monday morning Kali confronts Emma and Chloe and a nasty argument and falling-out ensues. Though she is no longer friends with Kali, Emma feels very manipulated by Chloe. When Chloe starts to boss her around, Emma snaps and falls out with her too.

All three girls are distressed and recount their version of events to their parents. Each girl tells a version of the truth which leaves out any poor judgements they may have made themselves and blames the others instead. Each parent feels compelled to act because of the level of distress being shown by their daughter, and so they contact the school to seek help and resolution.

Because the school uses the *Girls on Board* approach, the pastoral care staff do not rush to use justice tools. Instead, they listen to the stories told by all three girls. As they listen they use their professional judgment to decide whether or not bullying has occurred – they decide that this is not bullying but normal-if-painful friendship turbulence.

However, as the three girls are all distressed and there is a likelihood that their conflict might well turn into long-lasting enmity, the staff make the decision to call all the girls from the year group together for a *Girls on Board* session. Neither Emma, Chloe or Kali want their specific situation to be discussed and that is agreed by the *Girls on Board* facilitator. The *Girls on Board* session takes place later that day and the general principles are re-aired with the girls. The facilitator places particular emphasis on the key principle that when a girl or girls are 'in the water' (without a friend) that is a problem for every girl in the year group. That is not just because the girls are all kind people and don't want anyone to be unhappy but, perhaps more importantly, because nobody knows which friendship group the girl or girls will eventually end up joining. Each girl in the year group must consider whether or not to extend an invitation to the girl-in-the-water; each girl must consider the implications for their own group and their own sense of security of having an additional girl in their group.

Within a couple of days staff receive reports that things have settled and the girls have reformed their friendships. Staff have not interviewed the girls further or sought feedback on the effectiveness of the session but instead have looked to distract and normalise school life to give all the girls a chance to settle in their own time and in their own way.

In this story we see how important it was for staff not to rush to assume wrongdoing had taken place, despite parental lobbying. By applying the balm and salve of a *Girls on Board* session, staff have empowered the girls to resolve the situation for themselves. No one has been judged or reprimanded; girls have renegotiated their bonds away from adult scrutiny and retained dignity according to their own references. Not only have the three girls been rescued from further distress but the whole year group is better off as these disputes have avoided becoming dramatically entrenched.

The *Girls on Board* approach is a winner too; everyone in the community becomes aware that the session empowered a girl-negotiated resolution. In the future, parents of distressed girls will start to use the language of *Girls on Board* themselves. Rather than calling for direct teacher intervention, they will discuss with staff whether or not bullying has taken place and, if not, whether the threshold for convening a *Girls on Board* session has been reached.

Exceptions

No two girls are alike and so far this book has sought to explore and build on truths that can be applied to most girls. It is also important to acknowledge that there will always be times when girls behave in ways that don't fit the descriptions outlined here.

As girls grow up they become more empowered to explore their individuality. The various ways in which a girl might identify her gender, her sexuality and many other aspects of her identity may or may not impact the way she experiences friendships. Girls with additional needs and atypical developmental profiles will again bring their own unique experiences of friendship turbulence. What this emphasises for us is the importance of remembering within the principles of this approach that each and every girl is unique. Teaching young people about inclusion and diversity is a core part of every school's implied curriculum and the *Girls on Board* approach can contribute to this important part of school life. Our experience has shown that it is not necessary to adapt the approach specifically to meet the needs of subsets of girls. Some girls may listen to sessions and feel less able to relate. Nevertheless, they may well benefit from understanding what drives the behaviours of others. Nothing about the *Girls on Board* approach implies universality, neither is there an obligation to engage. Instead it offers a framework in which to examine common features of friendship turbulence to which each girl will bring their own unique perspective.

CHAPTER TWELVE

Conclusions

By seeing parenting from the girls' point of view, this book has set out to dispel some myths about the way girls relate to each other and their parents. We have revealed that girls generally want less advice from their parent and more loving comfort. They want to be respected for the relational skills they have, and not undermined and patronised.

Just like all of us, girls hate to be judged; they resent interference in the complex and ever-fluid dynamics of their friendships. For girls, parenting is about empowering them to find ways to be confident individuals within the group, whilst still bonding and blending. Girls need their parent to understand that there can sometimes be a fundamental tension in the ability to be a strong, independent individual and still blend with friends. Getting the balance right is something a parent can genuinely help with.

There was a crystallising moment during a *Girls on Board* workshop during the very earliest stages of developing the approach for schools. During a role play exercise, two 14-year-old girls were asked to enact a scene in which one would be a teenager complaining about complex conflict between girls at her school. The other girl was to enact being her mother and offering advice. The girl playing the mother listened briefly to the teenager's story and then interrupted to deliver a very concise, well thought-through list of precepts and advice. Her thoughts travelled from 'you need to be true to yourself', along the lines to 'don't let anyone put you down' right through to, 'all this will pass and you will barely remember it in a couple of years' time.' The speech was comprehensive and really quite brilliant - articulate, accurate, compassionate and undeniable.

After she had finished there was a pause while the girl playing the teenager thought about her response. It was classic and encapsulated so much of what I think adults get wrong when talking to teenage girls. Her response was simply,

'Yeah, whatever...'

APPENDIX 1

Bullying at School

This book is not about bullying. However, if you have turned straight to this appendix because you feel your daughter has been or is being bullied, you are not alone. Many parents assume, as soon as their child comes home desperately upset as a result of another child's actions, that they are the victim of "bullying". However, bullying is rare and the vast majority of cases of school-age conflict are within the bounds of normal friendship upset. This appendix will take a look at how we define bullying and why it can be unhelpful to label all but the most extreme examples of conflict with this word.

Conflict between girls at school exists on a spectrum ranging from mild, temporary misunderstandings through to clear acts of bullying and, rarely, criminal behaviour. Writing in the British Journal of Sociology in Education, Professor Jessica Ringrose of the University of London argues that there is a gap in the tools that schools use to support girls who are in conflict. She says that, when seen from the binary point of view of official school policies, girls are either happy or they are being bullied. There is no policy guidance for the conflict that might arise in the vast space between those two extremes. Her article ends with,

"In concluding, it would seem new conceptual frameworks for approaching girls' conflict are needed that critically engage with the limitations of the [...] discourses of aggression

and bullying, which dominate [...] policy and research."

It is our belief that the *Girls on Board* approach is this new conceptual framework. *Girls on Board* fills the gap between 'happy' and 'bullied' with a carefully prescribed method to support girls through friendship turbulence.

Ringrose goes on to describe the effect of using anti-bullying policies in schools. These policies can be blunt instruments when it comes to resolving conflict. She argues that these policies,

"...miss the complexity of the dynamics at play among girls and also neglect the power relations of parenting, ethnicity, class and school choice, which can inform how, why and when bullying [policies] are mobilized."

If teachers apply the anti-bullying policy because they have no other strategy at their disposal they can unwittingly,

"...escalate conflict and heighten anxiety and defensiveness."

Using the *Girls on Board* approach empowers girls in school to signal that they are being upset by the actions of others. Teachers can then assess whether or not to call a *Girls on Board* session. If called, the session will evoke empathy in the girls who, collectively, will seek to calm upset and challenge aggression. Bullying in *Girls on Board* schools is extremely rare.

Bullying and the law

The clearest examples of bullying are where behaviours reach a point at which we can say the law has been broken. If a girl has her property damaged, or is shoved or hurt deliberately then the law has been broken. If a girl's reputation is damaged by the posting of injurious comments and pictures on a public internet forum, then the law has been broken. If verbal or physical aggression is shown towards someone on the basis of 'protected characteristics' (race, ethnicity, nationality, disability, gender, sex, sexual orientation, religion and beliefs) then the law has been broken. These are all examples of 'acts of bullying' and are against the law in their own right. Depending on the intent and severity of the incident, the school may decide to take serious action against the perpetrator(s), including permanent exclusion, on the basis of just one instance of this behaviour.

However, under school regulation in England 'bullying' is defined as multiple 'acts of bullying' that accumulate over time: a seeming contradiction in terms. This means that your child is not being bullied unless she has experienced multiple acts of bullying such as those described above. This is generally very rare because it is well within the powers of schools to act firmly in response to this behaviour, before it becomes persistent. This type of bullying is overt; it is simple for the victim to describe and relatively straight-forward to investigate.

Verbal Aggression

There are other forms of verbal aggression that do not go far enough as to break the law and it can be harder to distinguish when they cross the line into bullying. For example, one child might berate another for any trivial difference, such as being exceptionally tall. Every day on entering a room or conversation someone might call them a name relating to their height or otherwise mock them in respect of it. Depending on the intent and severity of the action and the resulting effect on the target, this might over time accumulate to bullying. If the behaviour is clearly intended to injure, happens repeatedly, causes serious anguish to the target, and does not stop when asked, this is bullying.

Alternatively, less severe versions of this behaviour could be labelled 'banter'. Some mockery, verbal aggression and name calling can be jocular and reciprocal, forming part of their everyday interactions. Therefore, this kind of behaviour is not always easy to define and whether or not it crosses the line into bullying will often depend on the effect it has on the target.

Excluding behaviours

Parents might also be inclined to call behaviour 'bullying' when a girl feels she is consistently excluded from friendship groups. Certainly, if excluding behaviours present examples of deliberately and intentionally hurtful moments then a case for bullying can clearly be made. For example, if two girls in a friendship group deliberately tell the third girl they will meet her for a movie at the cinema, but then plot to leave the girl to be 'stood up' and instead secretly go to the bowling alley, this is an act of bullying intended to cause hurt. This exclusive behaviour cannot simply be explained away as *"we just thought she didn't like bowling"* because they have deliberately caused her to wait for them anxiously at the cinema, while sniggering behind her back at the bowling alley.

However, it can be much harder to determine whether milder examples of exclusive behaviour amount to bullying because each individual act can potentially be explained, excusing the perpetrators of any cruel intention:

- "We only didn't ask her to the sleepover because my parent told me I could only have two friends."
- "We didn't think she liked playing tag in the playground."
- "We thought she didn't like scary movies."
- "We thought she was in a friendship group with other girls."
- "We have tried really hard to include her, but she doesn't want to be with us."

Despite the many and varied ways in which a group of girls might try to explain their behaviour or waive away their responsibility for excluding another girl, the parents of the victim may feel justified in concluding that their daughter is being bullied: she is subject to behaviour that hurts her and this has happened over time. The problem here is that excluding behaviours are not always intended to hurt someone, even if they do. A girl – or a group of girls – may decide they do not want to be close friends with another girl, and this is not automatically 'bullying'. Girls are entitled to decide who is part of their friendship group and who isn't. It can be hard for all involved to accept, but we cannot expect or require girls to be friends with one another. What we can expect is kind, even empathic behaviour. They are allowed to exclude someone as long as they do so gently and compassionately. This is similar to the ending of a romantic relationship between two adults: one person wishes to end the relationship and knows this will hurt the other. The intention is to break up, not cause the other person pain, but the first thing inevitably leads to the second. Ultimately, if the exclusive behaviour is not intended to cause hurt then it is not correct to label it bullying.

As a parent, you may wonder where this leaves you if your daughter has been hurt by reasonable – if very painful – exclusion. In your response, it is crucial to understand that defining this pattern of behaviour as 'bullying' is unlikely to help the victim.

The Label "Bullying"

When you use the label 'bullying' to describe a friendship conflict, it has the effect of escalating the situation. By calling the behaviour 'bullying', you label the perpetrators as 'bullies'; this is a very strong word that implies inherently cruel intent. If it is concluded that the perpetrator is 'a bully', this has severe consequences for their sense of identity and friendships, and it is very difficult for them to regain their dignity. We should not forget that there will be reasons why a girl appears to have behaved in a cruel way and those reasons may well be centred around circumstances of which you are not aware. Simply calling her a 'bully' and sanctioning her is not necessarily going to make her behaviour go away. The outcome of an investigation into bullying may lead to a genuine apology and corrected behaviour; more often, in our experience, this form of adult intervention makes the situation worse.

On the other hand, bullying also implies that the target of the bullying is a helpless victim who has been targeted without blame and now deserves sympathy. For some, this position can be validating, invites compassion from the other girls, and can lead them to become more confident 'survivors'. For others, it is disempowering, implies weakness and failure and can have a lasting impact on their ability to understand and resolve conflict. Furthermore, if there is any element of doubt in the alleged bullying, the result can be that the other girls will regard the victim as having disingenuously manipulated the adults to believe that bullying has happened. Let's face it, none of us behaves impeccably in inter-personal relationships all the time and it is often the case that the 'victim' will have at least retaliated at some point. Ultimately, both the labels of 'bully' and 'victim' can be overly simplistic, problematic and difficult to recover from, and adults should therefore exercise caution when applying them.

Furthermore, once the bullying accusation is made, the school's anti-bullying policies are triggered, investigations may be opened, and the wider year group are likely to become aware of the situation. Parents of other children are likely to get involved and other players and historical incidents will be brought out. The application of the school's anti-bullying policy can be a crude tool that may well just make the situation worse rather than repairing the damage. Sanctions are more likely to entrench hatred and obstruct real reconciliation. Your control over how the situation will unfold is limited. Ultimately these layers of investigation and action do not align with the wants and needs of the girls involved: to build friendships.

Summary

Conflict between girls at school exists on a spectrum and bullying sits at the very extreme of that spectrum. Unless you are absolutely certain that the circumstances surrounding your daughter's unhappiness amount to bullying, you should think carefully before using that term. You should consider whether the application of the school's anti-bullying policy is likely to make the trouble go away or make it worse. It is important to focus on achieving a desirable and realistic outcome, whilst minimising the risk, drama and trauma involved for all. Our advice to parents who find themselves in this situation is to act on what you have learnt in this book and talk to your school about adopting the *Girls on Board* approach.

Social Media

Online bullying?

If the contact your daughter is receiving through social media amounts to bullying then her school will want to know and teachers can start an investigation based on the evidence you provide in the form of screenshots. Online bullying is taken very seriously and it is not uncommon for the Police to get involved.

If it is not bullying but nonetheless girls have fallen out on social media, the tools available to parents are limited. You can tell the school but there is often very little teachers can do to stop relational aggression happening online, outside school hours and off premises. That can leave parents feeling very exposed and alone in trying to support their daughter in the face of friendship turbulence arising in the digital domain.

The Internet

When a girl first starts to use the internet and a mobile phone the first thing a parent should be concerned about is internet safety. There are plenty of excellent websites and resources you can use to educate your daughter about how to be safe, like nspcc.org.uk. However, this book is concerned with friendships and therefore the question we have to address here is how best to support your daughter when fallouts occur online.

The debate about allowing access to personal mobile technology during the school day is ongoing but the wisest voices are surely those which talk about educating children about the *correct use* of these devices.

The age of social media has brought 24/7 communication into our lives. Social media networks allow girls to continue to 'discuss' their issues at all times of the day and night. It's a fact, it's here and it is not going away. Heavy-handed monitoring and harsh restrictions of social media use will not help or empower your daughter. When she is old enough she will need to be part of the same online community as her friends.

Guidance

You should guide your daughter in the use of social media as if it were part of teaching her how to look after herself; like you would personal hygiene, or how to get organised. Here are some guidelines you might share with her.

1. Be careful what you type online. Don't type anything you would not say to someone in person, face-to-face. Don't type anything you would not want a respected adult to see - like a grandparent or headteacher – because it is entirely possible they will see it.

2. Don't ever assume the person on the other end of your conversation won't screenshot what you have typed and share it with someone else, to your embarrassment.

3. Guard your devices keenly. Don't ever let someone borrow your device if they might then have the chance to 'jack' (= hijack) your social media account. Think, in advance, of some good excuses if your best friend wants to borrow your phone.

4. Never share your password. Sharing passwords is not a good way to show someone you trust them.

5. If a friend appears to type something which is uncharacteristic, stop responding and check at another time whether it was really them.

6. If you do get into an argument and you receive some nasty communications then simply say, 'Let's talk about this in person' and then disengage.

7. Everyone needs a proper night's sleep and you are no exception. Turn off or completely mute the device when you go to sleep; do not let it wake you up.

8. Never 'sext'; that means never share pictures of yourself which reveal private parts of your body or send sexually explicit messages. Sexting is never a good

way to form a trusting relationship with someone.

9.   If you receive a sext, you should delete it immediately and ask the person sending not to send pictures like that again.

It's a reality, not just a 'virtual' reality

It is very likely that at some point your daughter will witness or experience relational aggression online. It is as likely as it is that she will witness and experience the same thing on the school playground. By showing that you understand the true significance of her online world you can build trust and respect. Rather than becoming a source of generational disconnect, honest conversations about the use of social media can be a source of bonding between parent and daughter. If she shares the content of her conversations and posts with you, this can be a real insight into the conventions of her world and friendship groups.

You may personally disapprove of social media and therefore be tempted to want to dismiss conflict when it arises through this medium. However, just disapproving of the platform itself is not going to make the problem go away.

Use of social media is not a privilege; if your daughter is going to be fully socially integrated, it's a necessity. Taking away her access is akin to placing her in isolation. If she has broken some rules and you feel there is a need to sanction her then you need to consider whether complete isolation is proportionate. Taking away her devices is not like taking away her toys or games, it's more like forbidding her from speaking to her friends.

When conflict arises

We know that 'the keyboard' can encourage people to say things online that they perhaps would not have said face-to-face but it is vital not to panic when conflict occurs through this medium. Just as when your daughter experiences some relational aggression and anxiety at school, the same is now happening at home through her mobile device. It really isn't that different. **You therefore need to support the emotional subtext of what she is experiencing and listen to that rather than focusing on the words on the screen.**

Whose device is it?

It is time to have a rethink about social media and mobile devices for children. The argument that the parent is entitled to open access because he/she paid for and therefore owns the device is wearing thin. It is time to see access to this technology from the child's point of view and acknowledge the centrality of this form of communication to their lives. You might buy your daughter a notepad - that doesn't give you the right to see everything she writes on it. Mobile devices are personal and it is not unreasonable for a girl to expect hers to be entirely private. This is age-sensitive, of course; up to a certain age you may want to agree with her that you can monitor her accounts but there will come a point where her digital communications are hers and hers alone.

Is social media the real problem?

It is striking how often people complain about social media. We hear,

"If it wasn't for social media the girls would not be falling out with each other when they are at home. Home should be the place where they don't have to engage with all that stuff."

This may be true, but the use of social media is only going to increase. The genie is out of the bottle and we can't put it back. We have to learn to live with it and teach our daughters to manage it successfully.

It may sound trite but, it is not the fault of social media that girls fall out - it is what they write on social media that is the problem. Blaming social media is like blaming the invention of words. Remaining permanently mute is not the solution to human conflict; we all have to take responsibility for what we say.

Summary

Guiding your daughter in the best use of mobile devices and social media is a key part of modern parenting and this appendix has attempted to shed some useful light on the issue from the girls' point of view.

APPENDIX 3

Academic research

Here we quote and summarise some of the academic research that has been done into girls and their friendships.

"I know they are manipulating me..." Unmasking indirect aggression in an adolescent girls' friendship group.
Huntley and Owens 2006 International Education Journal

"Research has shown the damaging and extremely hurtful consequences of indirect aggression, leading some girls to consider leaving their school, or even considering suicide as an alternative to the pain they had experienced from indirect aggression (Owens, Slee and Shute, 2000). Very little has been written regarding intervention methods for this specific form of aggression. However, externalising conversations have been shown to be particularly successful in working with adolescents."

When Friends Disappoint: Boys' and Girls' Responses to Transgressions of Friendship Expectations
MacEvoy and Asher 2012 Child Development

"The generalisation that girls are more prosocial and empathic in relationships

(see Maccoby, 1998; Rose & Rudolph, 2006) *may not apply to situations in which a friend has violated a core expectation of friendship. Indeed, the pattern of gender differences in response to friendship transgressions may help to explain why it is that even though girls exhibit a large number of strengths in their friendships (e.g., shared intimacy, emotional support), girls' friendships are not found to be more stable than boys' friendships nor are girls more satisfied than boys with their friendships (see Rose & Asher, 2011). How children respond when a friend disappoints them may be a critical part of the story."*

'Just be friends': exposing the limits of educational bully discourses for understanding teen girls' heterosexualized friendships and conflicts.
Ringrose 2008 British Journal of Sociology in Education

"I [] trace some of the effects of bully discourses set in motion in schools to intervene into conflicts among girls. I suggest the practices miss the complexity of the dynamics at play among girls and also neglect the power relations of parenting, ethnicity, class and school choice, which can inform how why and when bullying discourses are mobilized...I illustrate how the bully discourses employed by parents and the school miss [] aspects of conflicts between girls, and instead escalate conflict and heighten anxiety and defensiveness...What is troubling is a school psychology literature is now amassing that takes girls' indirect and/or relational aggression as a premise for behavioural management and anti-bully policy...In concluding, it would seem new conceptual frameworks for approaching girls' conflict are needed that critically engage with the limitations of the psychological discourses of aggression and bullying, which dominate the policy and research."

Navigating Power, Control, and Being Nice: Aggression in Adolescent Girls' Friendships
Crother, Laura M, Field, Julaine E, Kolbert, Jered B. 2005

"The use of relational aggression is most likely a symptom of the systemic oppression of women through sexist practices. Within a traditional feminine worldview, the art and practice of assertiveness are often associated with promoting self-interests at

the expense of others. Traditional gender role stereotyping has created a narrow range of behavioral options that allow young women to be angry while remaining visibly "nice" in their overt behavior."

Friendship Features and Social Exclusion
An Observational Study Examining Gender and Social Context
Marion K. Underwood and Duane Buhrmester The University of Texas at Dallas

"As compared to boys, in the presence of the provoking peer, girls' aggressive friendship features were less strongly related to exclusive verbalizations but more strongly related to observed exclusive gestures. In the absence of the provocateur, girls' aggressive friendship features were more strongly related to exclusive remarks than were boys' friendship features. These findings suggest that the relation between friendship features and social exclusion may be influenced more by context for girls and that girl friends may dissemble more when excluding a newcomer, perhaps in keeping with their interpersonal needs for communion and harmony."

Adrienne Katz (Guardian 2002), executive director of Young Voice

"In the midst of such faceless confusion, many children abandon all interest in academia and concentrate entirely on working to be accepted by a social group...it is particularly traumatic for girls, because they traditionally need more emotionally intimate relationships than boys, which take time to develop".

Hereward Harrison, Childline policy research and developmental director.

"The bullying tactics chosen by boys haven't changed for decades, but girl-on-girl cruelty evolves all the time, taking on the opportunities afforded to them by new technologies, such as text messaging, and building on the tricks they learn as they go. Girl bullies are very creative and inventive in the way they carry out

their torture."

'Girls just want to be mean' NY Times by Margret Talbot

Talbot, Margret. "Girls just want to be mean". *The NY Times*. 2002.

Margret Talbot, a journalist, spent time speaking to Rosalind Wiseman (author of Queen Bees and Wannabees) about her research. She was also invited to attend some of Wiseman's classes and seminars. The article focuses primarily on gossip, cliques, ostracism and 'cruelty' among girls. The article then discusses the critical and psychological research conducted concerning girls and aggression.

The first main body of research conducted was by a team of researchers led by Kaj Bjorkqvist. He began to interview 11- and 12-year-old girls about their behaviour towards one another. The team's conclusion was that girls were, in fact, just as aggressive as boys, though in a different way. They were not as likely to engage in physical fights, for example, but their superior social intelligence enabled them to wage complicated battles with other girls aimed at damaging relationships or reputations - leaving nasty messages by cell phone or spreading scurrilous rumours by e-mail - turning the notion of the benefits of women's greater empathy on its head, Bjorkqvist focused on the destructive uses to which such emotional attunement could be put. "Girls can better understand how other girls feel," as he puts it, "so they know better how to harm them."

Researchers following in Bjorkqvist's footsteps decided to focus on girls as young as 4. They noticed that up to this age, girls were just as aggressive as boys (they snatch toys, they pinch etc). "Social expectations force their hostilities underground, where their assaults on one another are more indirect, less physical and less visible to adults. Secrets they share in one context, for example, can sometimes be used against them in another."

Marion Underwood, a professor of psychology at the University of Texas at Dallas, quoted by Talbot above.

"Girls very much value intimacy, which makes them excellent friends and terrible enemies. They share so much information when they are friends that they never run out of ammunition if they turn on one another. Some researchers have suggested this cruelty is about something closer to a hunger for power, even a "Darwinian drive."

Bjorkqvist, Kaj et al. "The Relationship between intelligence, Empathy and three types of Aggression". Aggressive Behaviour. Vol. 25, No. 2. 1999, pp. 81-89
On the basis of a series of studies, Björkqvist et al. [1992a, b] suggested a developmental theory of aggression. According to this theory, young children's aggression is predominantly physical. When verbal skills emerge, these may be used for peaceful interaction but also for aggressive purposes. The third stage of this development is indirect and manipulative aggression. Efficient indirect aggressiveness requires social intelligence, which makes it possible to hurt others by social manipulation. For instance, Björkqvist et al. [1992a] found that 11- and 15-year-old girls and boys used indirect forms of aggression more than 8-year-old children.

Currie, Dawn H et al. "The power to squash people: understanding Girls' relational aggression. British Journal of Sociology of Education. Vol. 28, No. 1, 2007, pp. 23-37.

"Girlhood as a culturally constructed 'way of being' is regulated by conventions that girls must be pretty but not 'self-absorbed' about their appearance; they must be attractive to boys but not seen to be too sexually 'forward'; they must be noticed and liked by the 'right people' but not be a social climber; independent but not a 'loner'; and so on. Girls' agency therefore comes from a culturally mandated

formation of girlhood that, although ever-present 'in girls heads,' is typically absent in adult concerns about girls' aggression.

The socio-cultural dimensions of meanness become obvious in the case of popular girls. As in previous research (see Merten, 1997; Simmons, 2002; Duncan, 2004), popularity was universally identified by the girls in our study as associated with meanness. Despite the fact that girls attended a variety of schools, popular girls were often envied as the girls 'with the power.' Somewhat paradoxically, they were also singled out as not well liked, primarily because they 'like to make fun of the unpopular people' (14-year-old Beverly).
In 13-year-old Vikki's words:

I don't like the way they lead you on. You know what I mean—like a boy does. Sometimes you think they like you, and then in the end they don't and stuff. So they lead you on in the friendship. You think they want to be your friends, but once you start getting close to them they turn away."

Merten (1997) explores how 'popular' girls use covert forms of aggression to manipulate peer networks. His research (carried out in the USA) addresses the way meanness is an expression of competition:

"Both meanness and popularity had hierarchical aspects and implications. Popularity was an expression and a source of hierarchical position. Furthermore, popularity could be transformed into power, which was also hierarchical. Like popularity, meanness could also be transformed into power. Hence, power was a common denominator between popularity and meanness." (Merten, 1997, p. 188).

Merten goes on, *"While 'popular' girls were typically described as the 'cool' kids in their school, 13- year-old Liv had a hard time telling us exactly what makes Popular girls cool:*

"It's really hard to explain, but you have to be cool. And it's hard to say what cool is, but you have to like wear the right clothes and talk the right way. Popular girls have to keep up their reputations because it's like if you do even one little thing wrong, it gets talked about everywhere.'" (14-year-old Vera).

Virtually all of the girls claimed that having attention from boys is a source of power:

Lydia: The thing with girls, if you have a lot of guy friends, that gives you power. Like Carmel: " ... She's Barbie. She's ditzy blonde hair. Like she's got a really nice body.

Jordan: The guys just fall for her because of her body. (Both 14 years old).

However, despite the admitted importance of 'sex appeal,' gaining attention from boys 'the wrong way' could earn even 'popular' girls the label of 'slut.' The wrong way was often —but not always — through sexualized appearance rather than behaviour.

Fourteen-year-old Amelia described a 'slut' at her school: 'She usually wears like these really, really short denim dresses with a denim tank top on and stuff like that, right? She wears lots of makeup and stuff. She tries to make herself pretty.'

Within this context, 'popular' girls, who have high status within school cultures, embody what Connell (1987) calls 'emphasized femininity.' As a result of their status, 'popular' girls are both envied and feared by other girls (but in some cases also despised; see Currie et al., 2006).

It may indeed be girls who police the boundaries of femininity through public gossip about girls' looks and sexual agency, they do so through a 'male gaze.' Boys do not need to be physically present to influence girls' behaviour; they simply need to be present 'in girls' heads' (Holland et al. 1991; Hey, 1997). Within this context, girls' meanness is symptomatic; that is, it tells us as much about dominant culture as it does about individual girls."

Comment from the authors: This is important when talking about the place boys have within the context of relational aggression and group dynamics. It is wrong, as proved above, to consider boys, femininity and heterosexual attractiveness as any more significant a factor than any other. Of course, boys may become a more significant factor to say 14-year-olds than they are to 11-year-olds, but it is just a different medium for aggression and does not fundamentally change the way girls relate to each other. Witness the strange culture that exists in some groups, of regarding an ex-boyfriend as untouchable and unapproachable by any girl in the social group for weeks or even months. This is not rational or biologically necessary or mimicked in adult life, it is a social construct created for use as a weapon for manipulation.

Strauss, Claudia. "Is empathy gendered and, if so, why? An approach from feminist psychological anthropology". Ethos Journal of the Society for Psychological Anthropology. Vol 32, No.1 4, 2004, pp 432-457.

"As earlier theorists (e.g., Burton and Whiting 1961) have noted, [...] girls can develop their gender identity as being like that of their primary caretaker, whereas boys' sense of masculinity requires negating identity with their primary caretaker. Compounding these different gender identity issues for boys and girls, Chodorow believes, is different treatment by their mother because mothers experience their daughters as like them and their sons as different from them: "Boys are more likely to have been pushed out of the pre-oedipal relationship, and to have had to curtail their primary love and sense of empathic tie with their mother" (1999:166). According to Chodorow, "Girls emerge from this [preoedipal] period with a basis of 'empathy' built into their *primary definition of self in a way that boys do not. Girls emerge with a stronger basis for experiencing another or feelings as one's own (or of thinking that one is experiencing a needs and feelings).*

Eleanor Maccoby (1998) argues that a primary experience for sex differences is that from the late preschool years on, boys tend to divide into sex-segregated play groups. Furthermore, boys tend to be larger and their play rougher than girls' groups. This gives the girls more practice in intimate interpersonal communication facilitating the development of empathy."

Comment from the authors: This seems to prove that girls have a greater pre-disposition to be empathetic. Girls are allowed and expected to express their empathy and that in turn makes them more practised and better at it. But at the heart of empathy is the idea that you take another's feelings to yourself – you literally feel them yourself. That is why empathy works in *Girls on Board* – because the empathy raising session, to a greater or lesser extent makes each girl feel and experience the pain of isolation that is being witnessed in the session. The narrative is:

We are here to do a Girls on Board session because that is what we do when there are one or more girls 'in the water' – i.e. experiencing isolation at the moment. Right now most of you are probably feeling like this isn't really your problem but after some empathy raising exercises you will feel differently because:

a. *The empathy will have amplified your sense of insecurity and anxiety about the quality and strength of your own friendships. You will want to help rescue and repair the friendship of the isolated girl in the hope that others might do the same for you one day.*

b. *You are now concerned about which group the isolated girl will join. Will it be your group? Is your group strong and secure enough to have a girl join you?*

The important leap to make here is that both reasons come down to self-interest. Empathy is not the precursor to altruism. The process of experiencing someone else's discomfort and distress through empathy, and the realisation that the situation of one girl's isolation affects you negatively on an emotional level is vital. In some schools *Girls on Board* is seen as unpopular by the girls as a restorative and empowering approach. This is because a *Girls on Board* session is not neutral. Girls realise that their friendship groups have some awkward decisions to make about where girls who are 'in the water' will end up.

Egeskov, Charlotte. "The Art of Masking: Women with Autism". Timo. 2019.

Girls tend to be a lot better at masking autistic traits than boys and some doctors believe that this had led to diagnosis rates in boys being 4x higher than in girls. Dr Wendy Nash (Stamford 2005) suggests that a diagnosis of autism in girls is often missed because the accepted symptoms have become male-centric. She writes:

"A lot of autistic girls get ruled out [of an autism diagnosis] because they may share a smile or may have a bit better eye contact or they're more socially motivated [than boys]. [In girls, Autism] can be a more subtle presentation."

Dr Nash also found that the brains of autistic boys and girls are not the same and that therefore the symptoms are not the same. It is not uncommon for girls who are on the autistic spectrum to struggle socially. Typically, people on the spectrum can find social signals harder to read, and can struggle with empathy.

Dr Susan Epstein, a clinical psychologist of the Child Mind Institute writes on their website:

"Girls tend to get by. They might not understand what's going on but they'll try to just go along and imitate what they see. And they may get away with it [up] to [Year 6 - end of Primary School], but once they get to [Secondary] school, it shows as a problem."

Brigid Rankowski, a girl on the autistic spectrum, writes on ChildMind.org

"People often remark on my social skills and wonder how I can be on the spectrum. I just laugh and remember the countless hours spent glued to my television mimicking the characters on the screen. My skills of echolalia and mimicry helped me 'pass' for years until the fateful day when all my coping skills went away. ... The thing I most often wish was 'normal' has always been my social skills. The social quirks I have of speaking what's on my mind and being completely oblivious are not always so charming to [others]. They can lead to depression, as I sometimes feel isolated in a room full of people who all seem to be speaking in a foreign code. ... The greatest thing a parent of a girl on the spectrum can do is to support her. Let her know how amazing she is and how much you believe in her. ... Most parents do love their children, but it is important to let them know verbally, because we don't always pick up on nonverbal cues."

"Females with autistic spectrum condition (ASC) may be better at 'camouflaging' or 'masking' their symptoms while displaying subtler behavioural presentation than males. Anecdotal clinical and autobiographical observations suggest that females with ASC show more social interest, heightened emotion or affective

empathy, increased imagination, better masking of social difficulties, different contents of narrow interests and more friendships than males with ASC."

Camouflaging or using social imitation strategies include imitations like "making eye contact during conversation, using learned phrases or pre-prepared jokes in conversation, mimicking other's social behaviour, imitating facial expressions or gestures, and learning and following social scripts". These masking or compensation strategies are often very exhausting for the individual to perform and come at a cost. Masking requires substantial cognitive effort and may lead to "increased stress responses, meltdown due to social overload, anxiety and depression, and even a negative impact on the development of one's identity."

"Additionally, studies indicate that females with ASC are more likely than males to receive a misdiagnose of other mental health conditions, such as personality disorders or eating disorders. Hence, the use of masking or social imitation strategies may lead to either missed or late diagnoses."